I love Andi and the message of freedom she so powerfully proclaims. I'm glad she has finally written this book, which will help you understand your identity in Christ, break free from the lies that hinder you, and step into your God-given destiny.

Christine Caine, founder of Propel Women and A21

She Is Free is a beautiful, vulnerable guide that highlights the importance of confronting your fears and limitations head-on. Our friend Andi marries her experiential wisdom with the Word of God to encourage others to remain immovably rooted in the unfailing love of God. The truths on these pages have the power to set you fully and completely free.

John and Lisa Bevere, bestselling authors and founders of Messenger International

Andi Andrew's book is an excellent portrayal of God's unconditional love for us and how we can choose to see ourselves in his image rather than believe the lies of the enemy, thereby unlocking our vast potential and changing our world for the better.

Dr. Caroline Leaf, cognitive neuroscientist

Andi is a carrier of the freedom that she has personally experienced and writes about in this powerful book. In a practical and transparent way, she vulnerably shares her path to freedom so that others can find their paths. I have had the privilege of speaking at conferences with Andi and have also had her in our Mercy homes. Andi is the real deal, and this book will change your life!

Nancy Alcorn, founder and president of Mercy Multiplied

We live in a day when truth is relative. Truth is presented as what you feel, what you saw on Facebook, what you heard someone else say. But there is a truth that stands the test of time, an unshakeable truth, and his name is Jesus. Pastor Andi, in her humorous, relatable, personal, and honest book, tells us how to courageously face our pain and how to overcome the lies that cripple and paralyze us with the Truth. We were created to live free and unashamed and to fearlessly empower others to live free as well. Andi is a woman on a mission who practices what she preaches. *She Is Free* has the capacity to practically and uniquely foster the presence and power of God so that women can grow in their faith and live out the purpose for which they were created.

Darlene Zschech

Freedom is contagious! Andi's passion for this message burned bright the day we met years ago in New York City. You'll find a fast friend in these pages, one who will champion for you and remind you what is TRUE. May these pages become a flame in your heart, as you step into the life-giving freedom that is already there.

Rebekah Lyons, author of *You Are Free* and *Freefall to Fly*

SHE IS
FREE

SHE IS
FREE

LEARNING THE TRUTH ABOUT THE LIES
THAT HOLD YOU CAPTIVE

ANDI ANDREW

BakerBooks

a division of Baker Publishing Group
Grand Rapids, Michigan

Published by Baker Books
a division of Baker Publishing Group
P.O. Box 6287, Grand Rapids, MI 49516-6287
www.bakerbooks.com

Printed in the United States of America

Library of Congress Cataloging-in-Publication Data
Names: Andrew, Andi, 1978– author.
Title: She is free : learning the truth about the lies that hold you captive / Andi Andrew.
Description: Grand Rapids, MI : Baker Books, a division of Baker Publishing Group,
   [2017] | Includes bibliographical references.
Identifiers: LCCN 2017018730 | ISBN 9780801093289 (pbk.)
Subjects: LCSH: Christian women—Religious life. | Truthfulness and falsehood—
   Religious aspects—Christianity.
Classification: LCC BV4527 .A53 2017 | DDC 248.8/43—dc23
LC record available at https://lccn.loc.gov/2017018730

Unless otherwise indicated, Scripture quotations are from the Holy Bible, New International Version®. NIV®. Copyright © 1973, 1978, 1984, 2011 by Biblica, Inc.™ Used by permission of Zondervan. All rights reserved worldwide. www.zondervan.com

Scripture quotations labeled AMP are from the Amplified® Bible, copyright © 2015 by The Lockman Foundation. Used by permission. (www.Lockman.org)

Scripture quotations labeled AMP-CE are from the Amplified® Bible, copyright © 1954, 1958, 1962, 1964, 1965, 1987 by The Lockman Foundation. Used by permission. (www.Lockman.org)

Scripture quotations labeled ESV are from The Holy Bible, English Standard Version® (ESV®), copyright © 2001 by Crossway, a publishing ministry of Good News Publishers. Used by permission. All rights reserved. ESV Text Edition: 2011

Scripture quotations labeled KJV are from the King James Version of the Bible.

Scripture quotations labeled Message are from THE MESSAGE. Copyright © by Eugene H. Peterson 1993, 1994, 1995, 1996, 2000, 2001, 2002. Used by permission of NavPress. All rights reserved. Represented by Tyndale House Publishers, Inc.

Scripture quotations labeled NASB are from the New American Standard Bible®, copyright © 1960, 1962, 1963, 1968, 1971, 1972, 1973, 1975, 1977, 1995 by The Lockman Foundation. Used by permission. (www.Lockman.org)

Scripture quotations labeled NKJV are from the New King James Version®. Copyright © 1982 by Thomas Nelson, Inc. Used by permission. All rights reserved.

Scripture quotations labeled NLT are from the Holy Bible, New Living Translation, copyright © 1996, 2004, 2015 by Tyndale House Foundation. Used by permission of Tyndale House Publishers, Inc., Carol Stream, Illinois 60188. All rights reserved.

Scripture quotations labeled TPT are taken from Letters from Heaven by the Apostle Paul, The Psalms: Poetry on Fire, and Proverbs: Wisdom from Above, The Passion Translation®, copyright © 2014, 2015, 2016. Used by permission of BroadStreet Publishing Group, LLC, Racine, Wisconsin, USA. All right reserved. ThePassionTranslation.com

Scripture quotations labeled Voice are from The Voice Bible, copyright © 2012 Thomas Nelson, Inc. The Voice™ translation © 2012 Ecclesia Bible Society. All rights reserved.

Author is represented by The Christopher Ferebee Agency, www.christopherferebee.com.

18   19   20   21   22   23   7   6   5   4   3   2

To my beautiful and only daughter,
Finley Grace

The moment you were born, it all changed. Your peaceful, beautiful, and joyful entrance onto the earth and into my arms during one of the darkest nights of my soul was a catalyst for freedom.

Months before your birth, someone who had never met us prophesied to my father and mother that I was pregnant with a daughter and that she would be a "flower" bringing beauty and life into a hard season. You did, and you bring that beauty and life to all that you do and touch every day.

Finley, may you stand on my shoulders and live free in your beautiful Kingdom inheritance here on earth as it is in heaven, connected to the deep Love of the Father all the days of your life.

I love you, Finley Grace, "from a blessed place"— with my whole heart that has been healed in the hands of the Father.

Contents

Introduction

I've heard it said, "What you don't know can't hurt you," but what I didn't know was destroying me. Ten years of serving Jesus on my resumé, knee-deep in three kids under the age of three, married for seven years, and yet I was completely unaware of how deeply loved I was by my Father in heaven. I didn't know there was no need to perform, serve, and achieve for love and acceptance or that I could live from a place of deep love and acceptance. I was one of the greatest Christian performers around, yet I wasn't getting paid for my efforts. I was desperate for the real thing, for someone to let me fall apart and see me in my mess and not walk away. What I didn't know was that Jesus was right there all along waiting for my great unraveling. Not only that, He didn't walk away; He gently and steadily led me into healing and wholeness.

How often have you heard this phrase, "The truth will set you free!"? Many times it is out of scriptural context. This line by itself is used in movies, churches, devotionals, and countless conversations around the world, but the truth alone can't set you free because it depends on what truth you're holding on to. Is it your own truth? The world's truth? Your neighbor's truth? Buddha's truth? The government's truth? Pop culture's truth? What about the truth of your past and pain? Or the shocking truth of your present reality that hurts more than anything? All of these "truths" will fade away, yet there is One whose truth is eternally unshakable because He *is* truth incarnate, the word made flesh. This is the truth that we can align our lives with to live in freedom.

> So Jesus was saying to the Jews who had believed Him, "If you abide in My word [continually obeying My teachings and living in accordance with them, then] you are truly My disciples. And you will know the truth [regarding salvation], and the truth will set you free [from the penalty of sin]."
> (John 8:31–32 AMP)

Scripture tells us that if we hold to Jesus's teaching—know it, walk in it, abide in it, and follow it—*then* we are truly His disciples or His students. Jesus only did what He saw the Father doing (John 5:19; 8:28; 12:49) so holding to His teaching and following in His ways is also holding fast to the Father's heart and ways. Once we meditate on and align ourselves with His truth, *then* we will know it and the truth of His goodness, love, and salvation that rescued us from the penalty of sin and death (John 3:16–17). *This* my friends is the truth that will set us free.

One thing I've learned on the journey thus far is this: our spiritual freedom is found as we learn the truth about the lies that have held us captive. These are the moments in which love breaks through the darkness and the blinders begin to fall off of our eyes, revealing the sweet freedom that is ours to walk in. There are spiritual forces at work that try to lure us into their world of lies. The Bible is very clear on this. In Ephesians 6:12, we're told, "For our struggle is not against flesh and blood, but against the rulers, against the authorities, against the powers of this dark world and against the spiritual forces of evil in the heavenly realms." Once we buy into those lies, they create an atmosphere or subculture around us from which we live, operate, and see our lives. Imagine the lies we partner with (whether knowingly or unknowingly) are like a dirty, scratched, and damaged pair of glasses. Glasses are supposed to help us see more clearly, but if the glasses are smudged, scratched, or dirty, our view is skewed. Lies do this; they cause us to see ourselves, others, and our lives without clarity.

Oftentimes, what's going on outside of us reveals what's going on deep within us. Whether it's the news, social media, circumstances, our spouses, children, leaders, friends, the driver in the car in front of you, coworkers, or that person walking down the street, any of these can push our buttons and squeeze our lives like a toothpaste tube. It's when we are under pressure that we see what is within us. Is it anger? Control? Fear? Unforgiveness? Or is it peace, love, joy, patience, and the like?

What if I told you there's a way to break free from the lies you've found yourself living in, that there's a way to step into the truth that is wrapped in love, enabling you to create the culture of the kingdom of heaven inside your heart and around your life?

In some seasons it feels like a fight to step into spiritual freedom, and in other seasons there's a beautiful ease in aligning ourselves with what is already ours in Jesus. I want to share with you how I've done this in my own life. It's an ongoing process for each and every one of us and, of course, a very personal one. It's a journey I hope we can share together. I believe I can help as a fellow traveler on the path of freedom.

So think about this: What if we stopped focusing so much on who we are and stepped into the fullness of *whose* we are? As we choose to crawl up into the arms of the Father, it's there, wrapped within His loving embrace, that we find a catalyst for an avalanche of freedom to take place in our lives. In His presence, we realize *whose* we are and, in turn, find out *who* we are. Jesus is our healer, and He has made a way into the arms of the Father and given us the priceless gift of the Holy Spirit to lead us into all truth (see John 14:6).

This book is about the love that desires to infiltrate the deepest part of our hearts and lives, healing our brokenness and pain until we place our feet on every inch of territory purchased for us by Jesus's blood. There is spiritual territory reserved for each and every one of us that is a rich inheritance in the land of the free. You don't have to just read about your freedom in the Word of God for the rest of your life here on earth, nor do you have to watch others bask in their redemptive potential while you sit on the sidelines—you can step into it, one step, one word, one moment, one prayer at a time.

You'll be equipped and activated to step into spiritual freedom by learning to distinguish between truth and lies. It doesn't matter when or where the lies have been spoken over us, to us, or about us. It doesn't matter if we consciously or unconsciously bit into the fruit of the lie fed to us by the enemy of our souls. Together—by sharing our stories and experiences—we will address the lies that surface when we partner with unforgiveness, fear, anger, shame, control, and isolation. We will then combat each lie with the truth of God's promises so that we can be empowered to step fully into freedom.

Every chapter in this book touches on another theme. Love, forgiveness, repentance, and connection to the Father's heart are at the core of this book. The greatest of these themes and the hero of the story is the unending, unyielding, constant flood of true love we each have access to in the arms of God. Freedom from the lies is available to all of us through God's Son, Jesus, and the gift of our helper and counselor, the Holy Spirit. We just have to be willing to do what it takes to partner with the truth and step into it.

As you dive into this book, ask yourself these questions: Is the kingdom outside of me dictating the kingdom inside of me? Or is the kingdom inside of me transforming the kingdom outside of me? Allow the healer to bind your broken heart as He gently whispers to you the truth wrapped in His love so that you can live a transformed life, free from the lies that have held you captive. It's time for the healing within you to produce an avalanche of freedom around you and bring the kingdom of heaven here on earth.

My prayer for you is found in Ephesians 3:14–20:

> So when I think of the wisdom of his plan I kneel humbly in awe before the Father of our Lord Jesus, the Messiah, the perfect Father of every father and child in heaven and on the earth. And I pray that he would pour out over you the unlimited riches of his glory and favor until supernatural

strength floods your innermost being with his divine might and explosive power.

Then, by constantly using your faith, the life of Christ will be released deep inside you, and the resting place of his love will become the very source and root of your life, providing you with a secure foundation that grows and grows.

Then, as your spiritual strength increases, you will be empowered to discover what every holy one experiences— the great magnitude of the astonishing love of Christ in all its dimensions. How deeply intimate and far-reaching is his love! How enduring and inclusive it is! Endless love beyond measurement that transcends our understanding—this extravagant love pours into you until you are filled to overflowing with the fullness of God!

Never doubt God's mighty power to work in you and accomplish all this. He will achieve infinitely more than your greatest request, your most unbelievable dream, and exceed your wildest imagination! He will outdo them all, for his miraculous power constantly energizes you. (TPT)

1

Trapped by Pain

For the Lord is the Spirit, and wherever the Spirit of the Lord is, there is freedom.

2 Corinthians 3:17 NLT

With my eyes slightly cracked open, I stretched my hands above my head, arching my back and exhaling the first pungent breath of the day. My hands slapped down on the other side of the bed only to find that Paul had already left for work. I lay there, wallowing in my sorrows and dark thoughts, buried under my depression, anxiety, and fear. I couldn't bear to confront the day ahead. Yet, at the same time, I felt a tension as desperation tugged at my veiled heart to break out from the blanket of heaviness under which I found myself. The trouble was, I didn't know how.

I felt trapped—trapped in my thoughts and emotional pain, trapped in a cycle of living that had me questioning my sanity. Too many times I had confessed out loud, "I feel like I'm going crazy!" and I was starting to believe it was true. I'm not sure if it was the postpartum hormones for the third time around or all the neglected pain that had accumulated over the course of my lifetime up until that moment. Needless to say, I was in turmoil, and something had to give.

I felt like a donkey led by a carrot on a stick, chasing an ever-elusive freedom always dangling in front of me out of reach. I had read about this freedom in the Bible countless times and had heard sermons about it, but it seemed as though I was the donkey destined never to reach it. Maybe it was for everyone else but me. Many moments of failure woven into my days solidified a fear in me that I might just need to live out my Christian life faking it, always putting on a show for everyone around me. After all, I had become good at it. I could keep hiding behind my sense of humor, believing this was as good as the Christian life gets. But the trouble was, I knew that wasn't true. If the same power that raised Christ Jesus from the dead was alive and at work in me (Rom. 8:11), then surely that power was enough to pull me out of this pit.

Something innate in me knew the greatness and goodness of my God and His ability to set me free. I knew that two choices lay before me: completely surrender my mind, will, heart, and emotions to an unseen God or succumb to the darkness I felt creeping in all around me.

As I lay there allowing the accuser to whisper morbid thoughts into my ear, the sound of my daughter's shrill cry interrupted the introspective spiral I had been entertaining.

The sound made my skin crawl, which was not the loving maternal response I was expecting. It was the reaction of a momma in pain. My daughter needed me. But even more than that, I needed to get out of the prison I was locked in so that I could be fully present to my husband and children and fully present to the life I was created to live.

A deep sadness engulfed every part of me, swallowing the very deepest places of my heart. I was so crippled by depression that I didn't even want to move at the sound of my daughter's crying. I didn't have the energy to swing my feet over the side of the bed, stand up, and go feed my precious baby girl. Instead, I rolled out of the bed and fell facedown onto the floor. There, the trigger was pulled. Uncontrollable sobs welled up from within the deep, dark crevices of my soul, and I let it all come out. Every thought, every fear, all my anger, shame, and pain . . . it all came out in a cacophony of wailing, whimpering, and deep guttural sobs. Dripping snot mixed with tears and ran into my dirty, matted hair. My daughter continued to cry out for me to come hold and nurse her, but first, I needed to be held.

In the midst of my sobs, I said over and over again, "I don't have anything but You. I don't have anything but You. I don't have anything but You," when all of a sudden a tangible peace entered the room. In an instant, I felt the presence of God hovering over me like a protective Father, Jesus kneeling beside me on the floor with His arm around me, and the Holy Spirit comforting me in an all-encompassing embrace. It was overwhelming and vulnerable, yet at the same time sweet and hopeful. Freedom had come knocking on my door in the form of the Father, Son, and Holy Spirit, and I let them into the hardest and scariest parts of my heart like a flood.

I wailed with every emotion and memory from the past thirty years flashing before me: moments of trauma, pain, betrayal, rejection, shame, and impenetrable fear. Everything seemed to be erupting to the surface of my soul to be refined in fire. It was a force I was unable to hold back. I didn't want to. It felt good to let it all go.

In the very moment when I felt alone and abandoned in a pit of darkness, faking my attitudes and actions like I thought a good Christian should, the lover of my soul came and protected me, comforted me, and knelt down beside me, wrapping His love around me like a soft, warm blanket on a cold winter's night. In an instant, I knew it would all be okay even though I didn't know how. My trust in the unfailing, healing lover of my soul was being restored. Somehow, someway, I knew I could be free.

I heard a whisper in response to my lament, "That's right, I AM all you've got. I AM here." And just like that, I knew the I AM was all I needed to break free. A new leg on the journey had begun.

After a moment of letting that revelatory whisper sink into my heart, I got up and went to my daughter.

No Wonder the Dam Burst

When I was very young, someone close to my family sexually molested me. It is a terrible thing at any age, but the fallout from those incidents affected virtually every area of my life from then on. I had an uncontrollable temper stemming back to some of my earliest memories that unfortunately followed me into adulthood. At times, I was confused and erratic, acting out for love and attention. My parents had their own problems brought on from their own personal journeys, which they dealt with in a variety of ways. This drew their attention from their children's hearts as they grasped in desperation to fix their own crumbling world.

I was an impulsive, passionate teenager and did things I regret. I don't regret finding Jesus at nineteen, but it would be a few more years before I truly grew into my relationship with Him, understanding the fullness of love and freedom that were mine to walk in. In the meantime, I fell in love, married the man of my dreams, and carried all of my undealt-with issues into the center of our marriage. Motherhood brought on bouts of postpartum depression that lingered well into long-term depression. Fear and anxiety swirled around in the pit of my stomach as I strove to cover up all of my imperfections. Work- and life-related stress and emotional pain brought on stress-related illnesses. It was a mess. *I* was a mess.

Finally, after the dam burst and while I laid there on the floor in my brokenness, God got my attention. I've been intentionally stepping into His deep love and words of truth and life ever since that pivotal moment.

Why Freedom? Well, Let Me Tell You

I would love to tell you that everything was fine from that instant forward, but this one moment in time was simply a tipping point for an avalanche of freedom in my life. While I had experienced moments of freedom and insight before, this experience was different. It marked a turning point that motivated me to protect the freedom I had received, while propelling me forward to understand more of the nature and character of God and his goodness with all that I had, come hell or high water (and both of those have definitely come while on the journey).

Lying there, utterly surrounded, I had an encounter with the all-consuming love of our God. The refiner's fire came to me in the form of an unshakable embrace that almost instantaneously brought the dross and dirt from my life to the surface. All the impurities began to come out of hiding in the safety of unadulterated love. That moment on the floor gave me a deep knowing that the very being of God—the One who *is* love—would purify me and that His process would bring the sweet freedom I had been chasing after in my own strength. In that split second I made a choice: I submitted my whole life to the process of freedom, no matter what it looked like. I was no longer afraid to look my pain in the face because I knew Who was with me.

As I lay there on the floor, I realized that in this union and connection with Him, His love was being completed and perfected within me. His love was a healing salve to soothe the inflamed, dysfunctional, and broken parts of my heart. This love was dispelling the darkness and fear I had partnered with, the lies and deception I had allowed to reside in me. This love is the shelter that deflects and breaks the arrows shot at my wounded heart from the enemy of my soul. In this oasis of love, it all changes. This is the gospel, the Good News that Jesus came to bring. We are reconnected to this love and being perfected in it to be bearers of His image (that we are all created in), here on earth as it is in heaven. The gospel encompasses all of our freedom.

The revelation came: when I purposefully still myself and meditate on the Father's endless love for me, He whispers to me the truth of my inheritance in Him to which I have unrestricted access because of Jesus. This unrestricted access to the Father comes to us just as Jesus said it would through His life in John 14:6–7: "I am the way and the truth and the life. No one comes to the Father except through me. If you really know me, you will know my Father as well."

When I simply become aware of His unending presence in my life, it's amazing how easily He replaces all my fears—which come out of a conscious or unconscious partnership with the enemy's lies—with His pure love. Oftentimes, we meditate on negative thoughts and disastrous outcomes, but purposefully abiding (John 15) in God and His love is the perfecting of our faith; this aids the daily cultivation of our freedom.

Our God is the very person of love, as well as everything else that is wonderful and good. He sent His Son, Jesus, as love incarnate on the earth to save our lives, release us from prison, and set us free. When we receive this as truth, we are instantaneously given the gift of the Holy Spirit to commune with and receive truth from. With this foundation, every single one of us can be set free no matter what we think, feel, or have walked through.

Whoever confesses *and* acknowledges that Jesus is the Son of God, God abides in him, and he in God. We have come to know [by personal observation and experience], and have believed [with deep, consistent faith] the love which God has for us. God is love, and the one who abides in love abides in God, and God abides *continually* in him. In this [union and fellowship with Him], love is completed and perfected with us, so that we may have confidence in the day of judgment [with assurance and boldness to face Him]; because as He is, so are we in this world. There is no fear in love [dread does not exist]. But perfect (complete, full-grown) love drives out fear, because fear involves [the expectation of divine] punishment, so the one who is afraid [of God's judgment] is not perfected in love [has not grown into a sufficient understanding of God's love]. (1 John 4:15–18 AMP)

Freedom Is a Work in Progress

As I build trust and connection with God through the years, the dross is scraped away, and the gold in my heart grows and is purified. The process doesn't happen overnight; it continues year after year, layer after layer, as God remains faithful to His workmanship in me. By wrestling with the Word of God and allowing Him to love, teach, and instruct me in His presence; by investigating and understanding my deepest emotions and the complex inner workings of my heart and mind with counselors, therapists, and inner healing ministers if need be; by talking and praying with trusted friends and family; and through the unwavering, steady nature of my husband, who consistently loves me even when I feel unlovable, I have been strengthened in the truth. I have learned how to wield my sword and persevere while conquering the giants that once taunted me and told me I could never live in what God has already given: *freedom*.

I've woken up to the reality that our spiritual freedom is fought for and won on the battlefield between truth and lies. Life gets complicated when we continually partner with the lies that come to steal, kill, destroy, and ultimately bind our lives in captivity. The longer we remain in agreement with the lies sown into our hearts, the stronger they can become, distorting our reality as we look through broken lenses at our world. The truth is that we are wrapped in and connected to Christ at all times—we are never separated from His love. His love desires to take over every inch of our hearts, dispelling the darkness so that we can step into the fullness of who He is (Eph. 3:16–19).

For years, I had known in my head who God was, and oftentimes even experienced His goodness. I knew what He was capable of doing for me and in me, but certain areas of my life hadn't been perfected in His love! To be honest, I'm still working on it—we all are.

No Substitutes for God's Presence

I love baking chocolate chip cookies. As a matter of fact, I'm known for my secret recipe. When I went through a season of health challenges, I stopped eating sugar and tried my hand at baking a few healthy, sugar-free things. I love a lot of the recipes we discovered on this sugar-free journey (my kids, not so much), but no matter what I try, there are no substitutes for the "real" chocolate chip cookies I make. Nothing compares to real salted butter and raw, organic sugars when it comes to baking chocolate chip cookies.

On the day I was scheduled to teach our interns at church about identity, I woke up with a phrase running through my head and my heart: "There is no substitute for the presence of God." This phrase repeated itself over and over again until it hit me: God's presence is the *one* thing for which there is no substitute. It's the one thing David asked for in Psalm 27:4:

Here's the one thing I crave from God, the one thing I seek above all else: I want the privilege of living with him every moment in his house, finding the sweet loveliness of his face, filled with awe, delighting in his glory and grace. I want to live my life so close to him that he takes pleasure in my every prayer. (TPT)

God's presence is the one thing that brings peace to our storms, answers to our questions, freedom to our minds, and identity to our fractured hearts. We must choose to make ourselves aware of His unending presence in our lives and to bring our pain to Him because He is the healer. You cannot earn His presence; on the cross, Jesus made a way for us to have access to the Father at all times. It's in the acknowledgment of His presence that He imparts His perspective, causing us to soar above our issues as we find healing in His arms—the safest place we can be.

In our personal journey to freedom, there are no substitutes for His presence. For years I looked to people to stand in Jesus's place only to realize that they were human and imperfect. Oftentimes disappointment, disillusionment, and ultimately offense and bitterness would begin to take root in my heart as I put people in a position to meet needs that only Jesus can. Then I would move on to other substitutes, which we all do from time to time, simple distractions that can become addictions in order to dull the pain within us: TV show binges, overuse of alcohol, drug abuse, food addictions, nightlife, work, perfection, performance, and so on. However, as crazy as it sounds, feeling pain is essential to finding out what needs healing in our lives. Our distractions tend to replace our face-to-face time with the

Father, who has the desire, ability, and power to search our hearts and help us face our pain and be healed. We have to stop trying to mask our pain with counterfeits and simply be with Him.

Feeling the Pain, Healing the Pain

I gave birth to each of my four children without an epidural or any form of pain medication. I'm neither morbid nor a masochist (I promise); it's simply a personal conviction, which I am by no means putting on you. Without pain medication, I knew what my body was doing. I knew the pain had a purpose, and I could feel when I needed to push. I was able to endure the discomfort because, at the end of the process, a beautiful child was placed in my arms, accompanied by an endorphin rush that surpasses any synthetic high on earth. Birth is this crazy, wonderful, messy roller coaster where pain and joy meet. The pain, in the end, was worth it.

After moving to New York and pastoring for a few years, some issues started to come up for me due to maneuvering through a few difficult seasons. Through a series of effective coaching sessions, I realized that some of my unhealed pain and even physical sickness were the result of unreleased, unprocessed, and accumulated emotions. I've always been a deep feeler, but for years I rejected a huge part of my identity, believing the lie that I was too emotional and should be stronger or more stoic.

I understand that not all emotions or feelings are healthy or productive, but they are real nonetheless. Our feelings *can be* indicators that tell us something about our hearts; they are extremely important in our journey of healing. If we don't give ourselves space and time to feel and understand what's going on, we tend to shove our emotions down into a figurative box, allowing them to accumulate there, while we protect our hearts with the weapon of our choice. Eventually the dam will burst—we just don't know how or when. Or our unchecked emotions may end up in the driver's seat of our lives, taking over many of our decisions and causing us to act irrationally. We will inevitably begin to operate according to fear-based motivators and surface sins such as gossip, slander, addiction, and the like that point to deeper issues such as unforgiveness, anger, shame, control, and rejection, which are indicators that our hearts are in need of attention and healing.

We've got to choose to live purposefully aware and attentive to our heart, soul, spirit, and body's needs. Only when we truly stare our pain in the face while holding the hand of our Creator, lover, and healer can we let the world we've manufactured crash down around us and allow Him to rebuild us the way He originally designed. It is in His presence that we can be healed and begin to thrive.

Do You Know God?

Maybe you've heard it said that there is a difference between believing in God and knowing Him. Laws, rules, performance, and outward appearance replace a deep and loving connection to an available God. Sometimes we even try to make our calling, purpose, or role in life our healer, and when that changes or the season shifts we're lost at sea. A lot of people would say they believe in God, but ask yourself: Do you truly know Him in a way that brings transformation in your life today? Or have you relegated Him to a man who walked in power two thousand years ago?

My brother Parker was preaching one Sunday evening service and said these words: "Maybe Jesus doesn't want to be famous. Maybe he just wants to be known." As Christians, we can spend our lives trying to make Jesus famous or recognized without knowing Him ourselves or representing Him before mankind. Such a relationship is like a marriage gone dry; you sleep in the same bed and methodically go through the motions, but devoid of connection and intimacy. The ring on your finger has become a rock instead of a symbol of covenant relationship. The truth is, if we don't live with a sincere awareness of our walk, the same can happen with Jesus.

When we are known by the Father and begin to know Him aside from performance, rules, and religion, and I mean truly, deeply, madly love Him and allow every inch of our being to be baptized in His love, we can continually walk in peace and freedom no matter what season of life we are in. There is no substitute for the presence of God. His presence is always there whether we feel it or not. You may not have an experience like I did with a tangible peace and knowing that the Father, Son, and Holy Spirit were right there in the room, but that doesn't change the fact that they are always with us. A lot of days I don't *feel* the presence of God, but my bond with Him is secure and deeply known.

Oswald Chambers, one of the greatest evangelists and teachers of Christ of his time, reminds us of the importance of being in God's presence on a daily basis. His words still echo today through his life lived in Christ.

We imagine we would be all right if a big crisis arose; but the big crisis will only reveal the stuff we are made of, it will not put anything into us. "If God gives the call, of course I will rise to the occasion." You will not unless you have risen to the occasion in the workshop, unless you have been the real thing before God there. If you are not doing the thing that lies nearest, because God has engineered it, when the crisis comes instead of being revealed as fit, you will be revealed as unfit. Crises always reveal character.[1]

We are transformed in the presence of God, in His "workshop." He has designed us for communion with the Holy Spirit (Rom. 14:17) so that we can become like Him. As we are changed in the secret place, it's essential that we allow our current season to reveal what's in us. Once we see the fruit released from our character, we must test it. Is it the fruit of repentance, forgiveness, love, or freedom? Or is it the fruit of pain, offense, bitterness, unforgiveness, or emptiness? Is it the real thing, or is it counterfeit? In His presence is where His spirit is able to reveal truth, uncover lies, and bring about our freedom: "For the Lord is the Spirit, and wherever the Spirit of the Lord is, there is freedom" (2 Cor. 3:17 NLT).

A Seed

I remember a time standing in the kitchen of our home in Australia, just months after I was that snotty, hot mess wrapped in love on the floor. As I washed dishes while watching my three little ones run around naked through the sprinklers in our backyard, my daze was interrupted by a still, small voice: "You're underground in this season of life, like a seed.

It won't be forever, but for now you're underground. In this season I will cover you and protect the work I am doing in you so that you produce the right things when you come above the ground, bursting forth with freedom. Let me break you, restore you, cover you, give you roots, cause you to germinate, and grow you until you burst forth with new life."

As these words flooded my heart, pictures of a seed underground flashed before my eyes. So much dirt and fertilizer—the mess, the darkness, and the stench. Water flooded the soil and fed the seed. I saw the seed breaking and roots going down deep. I saw a shoot rising from the top of the seed, heading toward the sunlight, as the deep roots drank in the water to bring nourishment to the rising shoot. I knew that this seed was my life, but I didn't know how long I'd be underground. God's measurement of a season and mine are worlds apart. The truth is, in that season, I was hiding from my purpose and calling. Being underground felt safe. I actually half-jokingly asked God if I could just stay underground forever. He clearly didn't feel the need to reply. It's good to recognize that we will all experience underground seasons throughout our lives—they are not one-time things. We've just got to get good at reading our seasons well, otherwise we will long for what's next without the resolution of what is happening right now.

See God's Freedom

As you read this, you may feel trapped by a barrage of circumstances, trauma, and pain that have brought you to this point in life with seemingly nowhere to turn. Maybe you're frustrated and angry all the time and not sure why. Maybe you blame others for where you are. In the recesses of your mind, there is a nagging feeling that if you start to address your pain, the whole house of cards you've built your life on will come tumbling down all around you. Maybe it was sexual abuse in your youth that you've never told anyone about. Maybe it was a conversation you had with your parents that shattered the perfect picture you had in your head of your upbringing, and now everything you've ever known feels like a lie. Maybe it's those few extra pounds you just can't lose that you're attaching your whole value to. Maybe it was the betrayal from your husband, the nasty divorce you went through, and the collateral damage you find yourself wading through. Maybe your parents abandoned you as a child, either physically or emotionally, and you can't seem to connect to people, so you perform for love and dissociate from reality. Maybe it's the continual rejection from men that causes you to wonder if you're valuable enough for anyone to ever notice you and (dare I say it?) marry you. Maybe the new season you find yourself in has brought the control freak out in you; you can't stop hurting everyone around you, and it's tearing you up inside. Maybe it was a painful church experience, the death of a loved one, the loss of a job that had become your identity, inexplicable pain that you have vowed never to speak of.

You feel trapped. The fruit of your pain is evident to you, and likely to those around you from whom you think you've been hiding it. You're starting to lose control. As you read these words, you realize you have nowhere to turn but God. Those "but God" moments are pivotal for your future: Will you live in freedom or captivity? You must choose which one. You may think your circumstance or pain has you cornered, but God is with you—His arms wide open.

Maybe you find yourself in a season where you'd like to remain underground forever, safe being unseen and unexposed to light. On the other hand, maybe you're frustrated that your gift is in seed form. Too often we despise the seed and want the tree it produces, now! We compare our "seed" season to someone else's "oak tree" season, ignoring the years of faithfulness it took for them to get there. If God gives you an underground-seed season, take it! Otherwise you'll try to produce fruit prematurely, and it will be bitter and inedible because it was produced by you and not by the process God has naturally set into motion.

As you embark on your own personal journey to freedom, you will need to allow for time in His presence to connect with the Father, Jesus, and Holy Spirit. If you value the fruit of freedom in your life, change your calendar, set your alarm, and begin the practice of His presence. Mark tells us,

> What else is the kingdom of God like? What earthly thing can we compare it to? The kingdom of God is like a mustard seed, the tiniest seed you can sow. But after that seed is planted, it grows into the largest plant in the garden, a plant so big that birds can build their nests in the shade of its branches. (Mark 4:30–32 Voice)

Make room for Him in a way that works with how you are uniquely created to connect.

After a while, it will become second nature to dwell in and hear from Him wherever you go, not just in the safe place of your home. Mark's tiny mustard seed begins to grow. You may not feel or hear anything at first, but don't be discouraged. Read God's Word daily and allow it to transform you. In the right moment, the Holy Spirit will bring His words of life to remembrance. Let me encourage you: "Draw near to God, and He will draw near to you" (James 4:8 NKJV).

Remain planted where you are, under the soil of His love and the water of His devotion to our growth. The process doesn't always feel good, smell nice, or look pretty, but we are each called to grow in Him and produce fruit so that our lives may be a refuge to others. Whatever you do, stay connected to the vine. John 15:1–5 tells us that our Father is the gardener who cuts off every branch that isn't producing life so that we can bear more fruit. He also reminds us that we cannot bear fruit by ourselves. Branches cut off from the life-giving vine are useless and wither away—remain in Him. Your healing will never come in isolation; it only comes in connection to the Father's truth and love.

Walking in Freedom

1. How do you like to connect with God? Take some time to think through how, where, and when you'll connect with Father God, Jesus, and Holy Spirit throughout the journey of this book. Are you someone who likes to journal? A thinker who needs time to process for longer periods of time? Do you feel things deeply and need time to give understanding to your emotions so confusion doesn't reign? Do you fly by the seat of your pants and enjoy the spontaneous? We are each uniquely made and formed for love and connection. Ponder how

you'd like to embark on this adventure with the Father, Jesus, and Holy Spirit.

2. Look at your schedule at the moment. How can you rearrange it to prioritize your time so that you'll be able to purposefully connect with God and become more aware of His presence? Maybe it's reducing the frequency of your nights out. Maybe it's setting your alarm ten, fifteen, or thirty minutes earlier than you usually do. Only you can change your calendar; nobody can do it for you!

3. Take a moment and write a list of the distractions you have accumulated knowingly or unknowingly over the years. These are the things that we do instead of facing the pain or looking deeper past the surface emotions or sin we operate in. Remember, distractions can be anything from TV show binges, a glass (or two . . . or three) of wine every night, food addictions, night life, work, perfection, performance, and so on. Before you jump into the rest of this book, consider fasting from your distractions and replacing them with meditating on God and His Word.

4. Think about buying a new physical copy of the Bible for yourself to complement your progress with this book. Dig into the truth, mark it up, highlight it, and write notes in it. There are so many amazing translations/versions out there that can really help the Word of God come alive to you: The Passion Translation, *The NIV Study Bible*, Amplified, The Message, New Living, the *ESV Journaling Bible*, and many more. Choose one and dig deep!

2

Chaos and Real Love

I will not leave you as orphans; I will come to you.

John 14:18

There's this moment each morning when our children emerge from their bedroom (yes, all four of them share one room) and slide into bed with their daddy and me. Whether for one minute or twenty minutes at the start of each day, all snuggled up together, head to head, heart to heart, bad breath to bad breath, wrapped in our arms—the connection we begin the day with is priceless. It's felt. There's a deep knowing we have of one another that is unspoken and needed. If I'm ever out of bed getting ready for the day before "snuggle time," you better believe that Sam is going to let me know about it. "Momma, why you out of bed? I want to snuggle you!"

One morning, I was staring at Sammy as he lay there glassy-eyed and groggy. My mind wandered to the fact that I have no expectations of him to perform for me or to say anything to me in order to validate me as his mother. I just love holding him. Connecting with him. Being with him. Looking at him. Hearing him breathe. Smelling his sweaty, matted hair.

I whispered to him, "I'm so glad Daddy and I have you. We love being your mommy and daddy."

Then he whispered back confidently and sweetly, "Yeah, you can keep me," as he turned in to snuggle even closer, as if there was still space between us.

In just the same way, our Father longs to connect deeply with us, and not just in the mornings or evenings when we schedule our "quiet time" but every moment that we breathe. He longs to fill every space in our hearts, not because He needs to be validated as a Father, but because He loves being with us.

In some circles, we've been conditioned to believe that our connection comes only when we put it in our calendar, but mandated relationship quickly becomes law and religion. The Father, Son, and Holy Spirit are always near, within, present, and available; we need only become more aware of what we already have. If we can cultivate an awareness of our emotions, we will be better able to detect signs of disconnection. This will help us in our journey to freedom.

What Disconnection Looks Like

The signs of our disconnection are quite clear. They usually pop up in relational settings and can be triggered by coworkers, friends, church leaders, spouses, children, or even random strangers. When we recognize these emotional manifestations—frustration, judgment, feeling overwhelmed or misunderstood, anger, control, shame, fear, bitterness, martyrdom, a victim mentality, and so on—and allow them to point to the underlying condition of our heart, they become lights that shine on a way of thinking not yet perfected in love. If we do not step into maturity, disconnection will become a breeding ground for lies to fester and multiply, muddying the waters of our revelation. When we are connected to the Father, truth leads to a deep knowing that we are loved in spite of the mess we may find ourselves in. Then we're able to throw out the unhelpful conditioning we've known that lies and tells us we need to have a clean, controlled exterior even when we're broken down and bleeding on the inside.

For instance, say a coworker disagrees with you publically in a staff meeting. Instantly you feel your heart beating in your throat as adrenaline shoots through your veins, paired with a desire to run to the bathroom so that no one sees the tears starting to well up in your eyes. It's possible that a simple everyday interaction such as this has uncovered a lie you believe about yourself. Perhaps you believe your ideas are not valid or don't deserve a place at the table. That moment may have brought up feelings of rejection or insignificance that cause you to want to isolate yourself from others.

It's important to get to the root of the lie so that we can pull it out of our hearts and replace it with God's truth and love. The great thing is, we don't have to "go there" alone because we always have the ability to be connected to God. When Jesus ascended to the right hand of the Father, we were given the gift of the Holy Spirit, which means we have full access to the powerful, intimate, and life-resurrecting Trinity:

> If you love me, keep my commands. *And I will ask the Father, and he will give you another advocate to help you and be with you forever—the Spirit of truth.* The world cannot accept him, because it neither sees him nor knows him. *But you know him, for he lives with you and will be in you. I will not leave you as orphans*; I will come to you. (John 14:15–18, emphasis added)

This is great news! You may feel orphaned, abandoned, rejected, alone, and left to sit in your pain forever, but the healer is with you, available to you, and ready to jump into the pit with you at any time to help you climb out.

Connection Is Doable for Anyone, Anytime

As you progress through the chapters of this book, taking practical steps toward walking in freedom from unforgiveness, fear, anger, shame, control, and isolation, it's important to see how simply you can do this in everyday life. Connection is doable for anyone—from parents with one or multiple children poking and prodding them day and night to executives working full-time jobs that demand they pull it together for their next meeting. It's possible to experience the freedom you long for and live in it at all times!

Allow me to illustrate with a story of an explosive moment I had with my kids. I wish I could say it was the first time, but that would be a lie. I adore my kids. It's just that sometimes they're like the flock of seagulls from *Finding*

Nemo saying "Mine! Mine! Mine! Mine!" and I am Dory being pulled apart on the docks of the marina.

In this particular episode of "let's peck Mommy to the bleeding edge," Paul was away in Swaziland, and I had just tucked my kiddos into bed. In that season, I was in the middle of grieving a betrayal that was affecting me deeply and oozing into many of my relational interactions—including with my kids. I had calmly asked them not to come upstairs for a drink of water, a question, or anything unless it was a true emergency—like, Mommy needs to call an ambulance kind of emergency. I had told them, "It's been a big day, and I just need some alone time with Jesus." Not seconds after my foot touched the top step, one of them was calling out for something that didn't require me to dial 911. Boom! I immediately started to shake with anger, stomping loudly away from the situation toward my bedroom so that I wouldn't unleash my wrath on them. I yelled out to the kids loud enough for the neighbors to hear, "Just give me five minutes to be alone with Jesus!!!" They quickly obliged and went completely quiet.

As I lay there on my bed, shaking, hand on my heart, eyes closed with tears spilling down onto my quilt, I said out loud to myself, "What's going on? What am I feeling?" Sobs welled up and began to pour out of the deep sadness I felt coming from my heart. I said out loud, "I'm sad. I'm sad. I'm so, so sad, Father." As I said those simple words over and over again, giving room for my deep emotions and grief, I was able to pinpoint where the manifestation of anger was coming from—it wasn't my children whom I was angry at. I was angry about the betrayal. I was angry with myself for lashing out. And I was sad. When it all connected for me, peace immediately began to flood my being. I allowed the Father to scoop me up into His arms and hold me in my sadness. He didn't tell me to stop feeling that way; He didn't curse me for being angry with my children. He just loved me where I was, and His love was healing.

Just five minutes later, as promised, I walked out of my room and gathered my kids around me. We sat on the floor together, and I apologized for allowing the sadness in my heart to lash out as anger toward them. I explained that when Mommy's heart is sad or hurt, anger or frustration sometimes comes out as I try to protect my heart instead of letting the healer help me. I explained that it's not their burden to carry. Sometimes, Mommy just needs five minutes to allow Jesus to come, be with me, and heal my heart. I asked for forgiveness from each of them, and in their different ways they lovingly obliged. Finley had tears in her eyes and couldn't stop hugging me, saying she forgave me. Zeke was gently stroking my arm and smiling with his beautiful gift of mercy. Jesse asked, "Who did this to you?" because his justice heart wanted to go and right the wrongs done to me. Of course, I didn't tell him but smiled at his zeal and passion. Then Sammy gave me his stuffed animal and told me, "You were angry . . . Daddy is really nice," and we all lost it with belly laughs. All was well. I had invited them into my healing journey, which was in turn healing for them.

I use this as an illustration of the simplicity of connection. At any moment of the day, in any season, you can step away for a moment, give yourself a time-out, and connect to the Father's heart. Maybe you're sitting at your cubicle, and your coworkers think you're deep in a project, but actually you're taking a moment to connect with God while staring at your computer screen. Maybe your baby won't stop screaming and you feel like punching a wall. Check on your child to make sure they're all right, then turn on some worship music and give yourself a few minutes to connect with Jesus. Let the Father's love into your anger, frustration, failure, rage, or sadness. When you've had time to calm down and align yourself with peace, go scoop up your baby and give them the love you've just received.

Connection Heals Us

In the place of connection with the Father, we receive healing, love, and truth. Lies are abolished in His arms. The secret place of freedom, breakthrough, and revelation is in connection to the Father's heart, and His intentions for you are pure and always good (James 1:17; Jer. 29:11).

One New Year's Eve, while praying over the year ahead, these words rose up in my spirit, as if I could hear a great multitude shouting out from the depths of their pain while I sat in a front row seat listening to their desperate pleas: "*See* me . . . *know* me . . . and *love* me. Truly *love* all of me even after you've *seen* all of me and *know* who I really am."

It hit me in that moment of intercession that every life is seeking love and connection in a world starving for attention. Just look at the desperate pleas we willingly share with the world on social media that scream, "Look at me! Am I beautiful? Loveable? Accepted? Good enough?" We live in a world so starved for affirmation that we're willing to get it by any means possible. These "highs" of acceptance we seek are merely Band-Aids to cover open wounds. They can only be healed completely by One—our heavenly Father, who has filled us with His Spirit to be transformed back into the likeness of His son, Jesus.

What does a baby need when they are born? Connection to a mother and father who are bursting with a fierce love that provides and protects at all costs. This selfless love brings forth an intimate connection that is both healing and safe.

The broken human heart will continue to grasp at feelings of intimacy and acceptance that pass in a moment and leave us emptier than before, unless we encounter the source of love. Maybe you're lonely and depressed. Maybe you never had a deep connection to your mother and father. Maybe a deep sadness is hovering over you that you just can't seem to shake. Maybe you're seeking connection through the temporary comfort of sex with uncommitted partners, or you medicate your pain and loneliness away with the substance of your choice. Ultimately, you are left feeling more alone. Oh, how this momma's heart wants to squeeze you tight and tell you, "You're not alone."

There is a heartbeat, a love and affection that you seek in the touch of another that can only be found in the arms of the One who thought your life was worth rescuing and dying for. You need only still yourself in His presence. Weep if you must weep. Tell Him all your thoughts and fears. Scream out the deep loneliness and let it be absorbed in His all-consuming presence. Let the Father, Son, and Holy Spirit envelop your being. Surrender your all, even if you think it won't work. Turn up the music so loud that it wraps around you to warm your soul like a thick, soft blanket on a freezing night. Stop thinking and feel for a moment. Give understanding to what's going on deep within you. Proverbs 4:23 says, "So above all, guard the affections of your heart, for they affect all that you are. Pay attention to the welfare of your innermost being, for from there flows the wellspring of life" (TPT). Let Him hold you like I hold my children in the morning. Connect. Know. Breathe. Lay your head on His heart. The attention and affection you seek is met with pure love in the arms of the One who created you and knows you. You are deeply known. You are deeply loved.

We have access to a God that sees us, knows our brokenness, and loves us anyway. Being *yet* loved after we are truly known may feel like a vulnerable place, but being alone is detrimental to the human heart. When we isolate ourselves from God and from community, we rage against all wise judgment (Prov. 18:1 NKJV).

Love One Another

Our love for God and one another will not only transform our lives but also the lives of those who don't yet know God. John 13:34–35 says, "A new command I give you: Love one another. As I have loved you, so you must love one another. By this everyone will know that you are my disciples, if you love one another."

I want the world to look at the bride of Christ, and be blown away at our love for one another. Not just a love that's lip service because saying "I love you" sounds right, but one that is seen in action. I want them to see that we're connected to Jesus and His life, not a list of rules. I want them to see what they have been seeking and not yet finding. I want them to find true love and connection in a world starving for attention, and I don't want them to just see it looking from the outside in. I want them to encounter it when they encounter me. I want them to taste and see that God is oh so good. I want my neighbors, the parents in the school yard, the cashier, the guy on the subway, the girl weeping on the street, the person who walks into church scared out of their mind that they'll be rejected . . . I want them to encounter the *love of God* by the words that come out of our mouths, the hands we've been given to serve and heal, and the life that we live in love and connection to the Father, Son, and Holy Spirit.

Love and connection with a God that sees us, knows us, and loves us and belonging to a community that demonstrates selfless love for one another will transform the world around us. We were never meant to do life alone.

Your Heart, Your Responsibility

In order to break the back of the lies we've believed, walk in freedom, and walk in connection with the Trinity and one another, we've got to take responsibility for our own hearts. We've got to stop expecting someone else to fix them for us.

I remember a time after we'd been pastoring Liberty in New York for a couple of years when I was very bitter and angry, blaming others for my insecurity and fear while continuing to perform for love. God needed to give me an eye-opening vision to wake me up from my pity party.

In this particular vision, I was wearing a blindfold. As I took it off, I saw that I was standing there with a machine gun in my hands, ready to execute a lineup of people who "owed" me an apology. They each owed a debt they would never be able to pay. Even if they broadcast an apology on

CNN, it wouldn't satisfy the need for vengeance I had built up in my heart. I was shocked at the degree of anger, malice, and unforgiveness that had taken hold of my life. My bitterness held on like deep roots infiltrating every chamber of my heart and causing it to harden toward the goodness of God. I didn't like the person I was in that vision, and I realized once again that I had to take responsibility for the state of my heart.

Remember, your heart is trying to tell you something— "As the face is reflected in water, so the heart reflects the real person" (Prov. 27:19 NLT). The emotional manifestations that bubble up in your life reflect the condition of your heart. Don't be afraid of what you see. In that particular moment, my heart was churning through anger and bitterness because I had thrown myself into the captivity of unforgiveness. I was simply manifesting the areas of my heart needing the freedom Jesus provides. Often we're afraid to face our pain, and instead we turn to behavior modification as a solution. In doing so, we refuse the grace of God to change. As we continue to mature, we are able to use pain as an indicator of deeper issues and allow God's love and truth to heal our wounds.

Psalm 139 conveys the depth of our Creator's knowledge of and love for us and His unfailing presence in our lives:

O Eternal One, You have explored my heart and know exactly who I am; You even know the small details like when I take a seat and when I stand up again. Even when I am far away, You know what I'm thinking. You observe my wanderings and my sleeping, my waking and my dreaming, and You know everything I do in more detail than even I know. You know what I'm going to say long before I say it. It is true, Eternal One, that You know everything and everyone. You have surrounded me on every side, behind me and before me, and You have placed Your hand gently on my shoulder. It is the most amazing feeling to know how deeply You know me, inside and out; the realization of it is so great that I cannot comprehend it.

Can I go anywhere apart from Your Spirit? Is there anywhere I can go to escape Your watchful presence? (vv. 1–7 Voice)

You see, we're never alone even if we feel as though we are. He knows us deeply inside and out, and we cannot be separated from His love.

Search me, God, and know my heart; test me and know my anxious thoughts. See if there is any offensive way in me, and lead me in the way everlasting. (vv. 23–24 NIV)

Allow Him to search your heart. Be intentional about it and allow Him to lead you in the way that brings about healing and wholeness. At times on the journey, we may need to seek professional help in partnership with the work God is doing within us. Things such as depression, mental illness, addiction, and so on can benefit from the insight given from a caring professional. (See the appendix for further guidance on this topic.)

Your Pain *Can Be* Your Platform

Years ago when Paul and I were beginning our church-planting journey, someone told us, "Your pain is your platform." Cue snotty, over-the-top sobs. In a split second, the lid had been taken off, and I realized that my pain, healed in Jesus's loving embrace, could actually benefit others. This revelation was overwhelming in the most redemptive way, and it brought about inexplicable healing. They were words from a loving, heavenly Father intent on binding up my broken heart.

We are new creations, though often we are catching up to that reality. Once we realize that Jesus has come to reconcile everything, including our created value and purpose, we begin to see that what we have walked through and what we've received in Christ can change the lives of those around us. We are reconciled reconcilers.

> Therefore, if anyone is in Christ, the new creation has come: The old has gone, the new is here! All this is from God, who reconciled us to himself through Christ and gave us the ministry of reconciliation: that God was reconciling the world to himself in Christ, not counting people's sins against them. And he has committed to us the message of reconciliation. (2 Cor. 5:17–19)

The truth is, our pain *can be* our platform if we are committed to walking through the process of healing, recognizing that in Christ we have become new. Sometimes, our pain is our platform while we're on the journey, even as others watch our lives being perfected in love. Please understand I am primarily referring to emotional pain that stems from a broken heart manifesting itself in our lives as unforgiveness, fear, anger, shame, control, isolation, and the like. Yet overcoming and being healed from any sort of pain can certainly give you a platform to change others' lives. We're free to set others free.

A platform is a place of influence that is given because we have something helpful to give away, whether through knowledge of a topic or experience from a personal journey. Note that a platform does not necessarily imply a microphone and stage. In a world where the bride of Christ is too often influenced by a surrounding fame-obsessed culture, we must grasp that true significance is not being known by the multitudes; it is being known by One and following the One. Any platform of any significance is birthed out of an intimate relationship with Father God, Jesus, and the Holy Spirit. It's a place from which you can lead others into a place of freedom and overcoming. As Matthew 10:8 says, "Heal the sick, raise the dead, cleanse those who have leprosy, drive out demons. *Freely you have received; freely give*" (emphasis added).

You may be wondering why pain is even a part our lives if we are loved by a perfect God. I need to be clear when it comes to pain: it never was or is God's plan or intention for us to experience pain, sickness, disease, or trial—He is good, kind, and all things wonderful and has been since the beginning of time. This passage in James tells us how to discern what is from God:

> Blessed is the one who perseveres under trial because, having stood the test, that person will receive the crown of life that the Lord has promised to those who love him. When tempted, no one should say, "God is tempting me." For God cannot be tempted by evil, nor does he tempt anyone; but each person is tempted when they are dragged away by their own evil desire and enticed. Then, after desire has conceived, it gives birth to sin; and sin, when it is full-grown, gives birth

to death. Don't be deceived, my dear brothers and sisters. Every good and perfect gift is from above, coming down from the Father of the heavenly lights, who does not change like shifting shadows. (1:12–17)

You see, God does not tempt or entice us into sin, nor does He give us sickness or pain; it's not in His nature—He is the very being of love. What He can do is take what the enemy has used to rob, kill, and destroy our lives and bring about abundant life where pain used to run rampant (John 10:10). I have seen Him time and time again work all things together for the good of those who love Him (Rom. 8:28). Our pain can be our platform if we are willing to give God our pain and walk into healing. We can walk in authority because we've gone "there" with God and have overcome.

We were made for God's pleasure—for relationship and love. We only need to go back to the Garden of Eden in the beginning of the book of Genesis to see that the original plan before the fall was love and connection to our Creator. If you have gone through pain due to the effects of a fallen world or are experiencing pain in any way, He sent His Son to bind up your broken heart and heal your body so that the enemy's authority over you in any way loses its power. Partner with that truth! He wants us to be free and solid in our faith so that we can become love for others. With that as our motivation, the weight of influence—that is, a platform—can be borne without a collapse of integrity.

If you're suffering in pain and isolation, I want to encourage you that your pain *can* have purpose when it's connected and healed in the Father's perfect love. We have the power to choose each day to partner with God and bring Him our pain.

Walking in Freedom

1. Take a moment to still yourself. Find a safe and quiet place to do so. What things or people have been pushing your buttons lately? What are your emotional manifestations trying to tell you about what's going on deep within your heart?

2. Take those things that are going on deep within you and invite the Holy Spirit into this moment. What do you feel, hear, or see? Take your time. If you feel stuck, don't be hard on yourself; simply ask for peace and clarity. Find rest in this moment.

3. Read Psalm 139 in a translation that comes alive to you. How does this Scripture passage resound with you? Does it feel like a distant truth that is hard to believe? Does it make you angry because you've never experienced this type of closeness with God? Does it comfort you and make you feel safe? Take a moment and write out your impressions. What revelation, if any, are you getting from this passage of Scripture?

4. Over the period of time that it takes you to read this book, commit to waking up in the morning and speaking out Psalm 139:23–24 as your own prayer for God to search and know your heart in this journey to freedom. It says, "Search me, God, and know my heart; test me and know my anxious thoughts. See if there is any offensive way in me, and lead me in the way everlasting." May He guide you into all truth daily, as you are reconciled because of His love.

3

From a Prison to a Palace

Let me be clear, the Anointed One has set us free—not partially, but completely and wonderfully free! We must always cherish this truth and stubbornly refuse to go back into the bondage of our past.

Galatians 5:1 TPT

The tightening of anxiety in my stomach ate at my insides as I packed my bags. I was nervous about leaving my kids for ten days straight as my husband and I flew off to Italy for the trip of a lifetime. Yet, I couldn't wait to leave. The relaxation, rest, and uninterrupted face-to-face time with my husband were gladly welcomed. We had moved to New York four years earlier and had only been away together for one weekend since the move. In the time leading up to this monumental trip, we had planted a church with three growing communities in New York City and welcomed our fourth child into the world. There were no signs of life slowing down.

As I wrestled with all of the justifications for this trip, "mom guilt" slowly crept in. It took a forceful effort to step away from the assault of condemnation so I could focus on packing my bags and boarding an airplane with my love. My four babies were very happily staying with my mom and dad. The only tears shed as we all said good-bye were my own.

The moment we landed in Rome, I decided to do a full reset. Knowing my kids were happy and thriving back home with their grandparents allowed me to completely enjoy the trip. We did everything an average Roman tourist would do: saw the Colosseum and the Spanish Steps, ate gelato, and ate more gelato. We walked through Ancient Rome and read every plaque we found, drinking in ancient history as often as we could. We saw the temples, the Arch of Constantine, the crumbling aqueducts, St. Peter's Basilica, the Sistine Chapel, and ate more gelato and pasta.

On our last evening in Rome, we made plans to see Mamertine Prison the following morning. A friend from New York City had told us that the prison in which the apostle Paul had written many of his Epistles was a must. We packed our bags that evening in preparation for the journey ahead to Ana Capri.

I woke up the next morning with a sober expectation that this was going to be a pivotal day. We mapped out the walk to the prison and discovered it was only five minutes from our hotel. We set out on our journey, hand in hand, silent, pondering what we were about to behold. We walked down a narrow set of steps approaching the Roman Forum beneath Palatine Hill at the bottom of the "sacred road." We reached the bottom of the stairwell, and to the left was a small door into a minuscule room fit with posters and a small sign that read Mamertine Prison. No line, no fanfare, just a humble door that opened our eyes to the prison whose dank, damp walls witnessed words flowing from heaven to an impassioned man obediently recording each of them in his commitment to the church that Christ had so recently purchased with His perfect blood. These words echo throughout eternity and have deeply transformed my life and the lives of countless others.

I saw a sign stating that tours start at 11 a.m., but it was only 9 a.m. My heart sank. I knew we had limited time to find a cab, catch our train, and make our ferry connection to Capri on time. Humbled by the reality of our surroundings, we quietly asked the woman at the counter, "Are we able to go in and see the prison? We have a train to catch and cannot wait until 11 a.m."

She paused for a few seconds, gazing back with blank, emotionless eyes. Her response was dull, but favorable. "Well, normally I would make you wait for a tour . . . but, yes, I will let the two of you go down. I'll give you a personal tour."

A Life-Changing Experience

My soul was dancing inside me, but I played it cool, unwilling to risk a change in favor with our rigid tour guide. We placed our four Euro in the donation container and followed her down the steps into the prison.

The moment I placed my foot on the steps, I began to do the silent ugly-cry. I tried my best to exercise restraint, but violent sniffles and uncontrollable tears rolled down my face, echoing against the prison walls. I was well and truly overwhelmed. In that moment, the tangible presence of God rested upon us, and I was aware of it for the rest of the day.

The room we entered used to be an old cistern that the Romans had turned into a prison. Convicts were lowered down through a small hole in the roof to a dark, circular room no larger than twenty feet in diameter. As we gazed reverently around the room, we spotted the column that Paul was chained to, where out of his passion for Jesus and pure desire to see the gospel advance, he wrote letters of instruction and encouragement to the churches he had planted, opening their eyes to see the truth of the Good News available to all.

I didn't know what to do. Was I supposed to cross my head, heart, and shoulders in the name of the Father, Son, and Holy Spirit? Sing a hymn? Get down on my knees and pray? Pull out my Bible and journal for some quiet time? All I could manage was to sit there, overwhelmed by this man who had suffered here as he passionately recorded words from the Holy Spirit that eventually constituted much of the Book that has changed my life—not to mention human history—more than any other in existence. We stood there in silent awe, lacking words to describe all that we were experiencing. Too soon, the moment was over. We needed to go.

We stood outside, personal tour complete, looking over Ancient Rome at the place where Julius Caesar's murdered body was laid to rest. As I gazed across the old city, I imagined Paul being dragged past the temples, each designated to a pagan god, flogged and mocked for his passion for Jesus, and then lowered into the prison behind me. I was overwhelmed yet again. A fresh passion to read the Word of God came alive in me. Any laziness or apathy toward my God-given inheritance to delve into the Bible left me. I couldn't wait to go and read my Bible again.

I shook myself out of the beautiful haze I was in as we ran to our hotel to grab our bags and catch a cab. By the time we got to the train station, I was nauseated from the cab ride. The polarizing contrast of our new environment with the peaceful presence of the prison put me in shock. We walked through the doors and were overwhelmed by scammers asking us if we needed "help" carrying our bags or buying tickets. Paul politely yet firmly declined.

A Visit to Heaven on Earth

Eventually, we got our tickets and boarded the train and then took a ferry from Naples to our final destination. When we arrived in Capri, we stepped off the ferry and straight into heaven. I have never seen anything more beautiful than the island of Capri. Colorful boats lined the shore, bouncing on the small waves of pristine blue water lapping against the pebble beach. The shops were bustling and the chatter of conversations taking place in the open-air cafés sounded like a serene symphony that brought rest to my soul.

As I looked up, my eyes scanned the mountains filled with fruitful lemon trees and tomato plants bursting with ripe tomatoes. My mouth began to water at the thought of the multiple Caprese salads I would consume in my time on the island. I needed someone to pinch me just to make sure I wasn't dreaming because surely it wasn't real. People really don't live in a place so magical, right? I mean, I had started my day off in a prison, had just been on an irritating journey (to say the least) to get to my destination, and now I was standing in this breathtakingly beautiful place. I was spinning again. The extremes of the day were becoming a bit too much to take in.

We booked into a hotel that friends of ours had recommended called The Palace. When we had looked into it online, the pricing nearly gave us a heart attack, so we swiftly reserved the only room within our budget—it was essentially equivalent to a servant's quarters without a view. At the end of the pier, our drivers, garbed all in white, stood awaiting us with exceptional poise. "Mr. and Mrs. Andrew?"

"Um, yes, that's us."

"Come with us. We'll get your luggage."

Yet again overwhelmed, and trying to take in all of the breathtaking scenery, we were led to a pristine, white van with leather seats and handed bottled water poured into embossed glasses for the journey up to the main town at the top of the island, Ana Capri.

When we got to our hotel, we were led to the front desk to check in, I was afraid to touch anything in my sight—it was all beautiful, perfectly maintained, and way above our pay grade. I felt like a three-year-old in a china shop; I just didn't belong. I was distracted from being present in my picturesque reality by a deep feeling that I didn't deserve to be in this place.

When we got to the counter, the hotel concierge checked us in and then whispered with a huge smile that she had a surprise for us. "An upgrade . . . a very nice upgrade."

Okay, surely she had the wrong people. But no, the upgrade really was for us. They escorted us upstairs to our room, and when they opened the doors I tried not to fall over. It was bigger than our entire NYC apartment, complete with a coastal view that took our breath away and overlooking a perfect Italian sunset!

When the bellman walked out of the room, I fell onto the bed, allowing the waves of emotion from the day to roll over me. I was trying to process why this incredible gift was so distressing, when really I should have been giddy with excitement. Why did I feel like I didn't deserve this? It felt wrong to be in this beautiful, elaborate room in a hotel called The Palace when my day had begun in a literal prison.

I'm Not Sure I Deserve This

Looking up to heaven from the comfort of my plush, king-size bed, I bared my heart out loud: "I'm not comfortable with this, God. It's overwhelming. Starting your day in a prison then ending in a luxury hotel that's not just like a palace, it's called The Palace? I can't handle this."

Then I shut my mouth as the internal process began.

"Why am I so uncomfortable with this? Why don't I like being lavished with God's love? Why don't I ask Him for more? Why am I more comfortable getting revelation in the prison than I am in the palace? Why do I have an aversion to being treated well? Why do I feel like I don't deserve an upgrade, but everyone else on the planet does? Why do I feel like I have to apologize for taking a romantic vacation with my husband? Why does it feel more spiritual to talk about my experience in Paul's prison than it does to talk about our upgraded hotel room? God, why do I care so much about what people think about me? God, being in the palace feels like a prison because I can't enjoy it . . . why?!"

Then I heard God speaking to me, as clear as day: "*Andi, all of your life you have been serving the God of Just Enough, but I am the God of More than Enough. I can take you from a prison to a palace in just one day if you'll go with Me. Sometimes it's a difficult, even irritating journey, but I have a place for you at My table.*"

In that moment, the inadequacy, pride, poverty mentality, and false humility that I had been unknowingly operating under for years was revealed. I cycled back to the memories of growing up in my family having just enough—and I was fine with that. It felt more righteous to stay in that frame of mind in my heart and life. Without knowing it, I had believed a lie that it was selfish to dream big or, dare I say it, even want for more. My parents were hard workers, and we weren't poor growing up, but we definitely weren't rich. Similarly, in my marriage with Paul, we have never gone without, but we've never lived extravagantly by any means, so staying in The Palace was messing with me.

Whenever "more" came up, I have always subconsciously labeled myself as undeserving—never expecting too much of God's desires for my life, including his promises of freedom. In order to avoid disappointment, I hoped little. "I'll have 'just enough' my whole life, thank you very much. Just enough healing, just enough miracles, just enough finances, just enough joy . . ."

I believed a lie that others deserved more, but I didn't. I had unknowingly allowed this belief system to seep into many areas of my life, and it had kept me trapped in a "just enough" cycle of living.

I heard a whisper from heaven interrupt my thoughts: "*I need you to be comfortable in the palace, because it is a place of authority, and it is for others. Andi, you need to understand that what you allow Me to do within you in the prison and on the journey will transform and ready you for authority in the palace. I will deliver you from the prison and lead you on a journey to the palace. And yes, the palace is for you, because I love you and desire to lavish that love upon you tangibly. Just know that the palace is also for others, and you must bring them with you.*"

I was reeling. This day was too much to take in, too much to handle, yet at the same time, I gratefully welcomed this fresh revelation. At the end of a tumultuous day, the cool breeze of the Holy Spirit was bringing peace and truth again. I realized I needed to keep putting one foot in front of the other while continually stepping into my authority as a daughter of the King, who's called to the palace of my inheritance to see others reconciled and rescued in kind.

Are You in a Prison?

This emotionally heightened day, taking us from Paul's prison in Rome to The Palace Hotel in Ana Capri, became a priceless allegory about the journey our Father desires to go on with us. God was using an external and material blessing to illustrate within me a deeper reality. *He* is our very great reward, the upgrade wasn't (Gen. 15:1). When man fell into the hands of the enemy in the Garden of Eden, the rescue plan—Jesus—was conceived in heaven and birthed on earth to pay the ransom for our lives. This is the underpinning story of redemption. His blood and His bruised and broken body paid the bail money to get us out of prison, so we could sit at the table in the palace with our Lord and king. The greatest act of love brought us into the family as heirs to all that is His (Rom. 8:17).

I love the Gospel of John. On several occasions John refers to himself as "the one whom Jesus loved"—that was some revelation! He had such an understanding and a knowing of how loved he truly was by Jesus, and it shows throughout the Gospels. In the epistle of 1 John, he says, "God is love. This is how God showed his love among us: He sent his one and only Son into the world that we might live through him. This is love: not that we loved God, but that he loved us and sent his Son as an atoning sacrifice for our sins" (4:8b–10).

There are mindsets of insecurity, unworthiness, and fear-based living brought on by unhealed pain that keep us trapped in "our prisons," unwilling or unable to go on the journey to freedom. False mindsets that have bought into lies come from living under the fall of man instead of living from love.

We don't have to work for love; we get to live *from* it because we already have all of God's love and cannot be separated from it (Rom. 8:38–39). God is love, and when we receive His Son, we also receive this life-giving love. My own deception was to unknowingly believe the lie that I wasn't worth the love that desired to heal and transform me while all the while toiling for acceptance. God's love releases us from the prison—this is good news! And we are already found worthy of His love!

Love is our greatest weapon and shelter. If you are willing, the Holy Spirit will shine a light on your unhealthy ways of thinking, open the door for you to choose new mindsets, and empower you with the grace to change. This is the privilege and responsibility we each have been gifted with: to ascend to and dwell in the palace where our inheritance lies. It's all ours; we just have to be willing to go on the journey.

There is a table that has been prepared for us. It is an invitation to His presence, for which there is no substitute. It is God's desire to release us from captivity, rescue us, and lead us on a journey to wholeness as His heirs. Be aware that most of the time this voyage comes in the form of a day-to-day, irritating, in-your-face-until-you-deal-with-it sort of journey, but it's so worth it. At the King's table we find our true identity and are taught to live from love instead of for love so that we may be moved with compassion to bring others with us. Godly love received is far too abundant to keep to ourselves—we are set free to help set others free.

The psalmist was aware of this abundance: "You prepare a table before me in the presence of my enemies. You anoint my head with oil; my cup overflows. Surely your goodness and love will follow me all the days of my life, and I will dwell in the house of the LORD forever" (Ps. 23:5–6). I love how God shows off His abundance to our enemies, preparing a table full of all that He has for us and displaying His overflow in our lives. There is so much rest and peace in that!

Our enemies are not a threat to Jesus because He is Lord. The storm comes to the wise and the foolish (Matt. 7:24–27) in order to destroy what is being built in their lives. Having Jesus doesn't mean we won't have storms; having Jesus means we are unshaken by them.

If you find yourself in a prison of broken-down mindsets or fear-based living, a trip to "the palace" containing your freedom is in order. And the good news is, it's already paid for.

We Have a Choice

Family dinner in our house can get pretty crazy. There's laughter, stories, interruptions, prayer, life decisions, jokes, inappropriate behavior (the phrases "butt cheek" and "booty" come from our youngest more times than I'd like to admit), tears, discipline, encouragement, and, of course, food. The table is a place where we engage as a family. Our children get to tell stories and discuss what's important to them, as do we. We talk about our highs and lows of the day and encourage each other as we go around the table. We teach our kids that interrupting doesn't bring honor and that some behavior is not for the table. Sometimes, a poor attitude or poor behavior will keep one of our children from coming to the table until they are ready to engage. They know that there is always a place for them there; they are a part of the family.

In order to step into the fullness and freedom of what God has for every one of us, we need to cultivate a willingness to approach His table and engage with family. There will be laughter, tears, encouragement, confrontation, life decisions, and, most of all, a safe place for you to be yourself in the presence of God. At the table, you will learn your identity as a son or daughter of the Most High God. But you have to choose whether you're willing to come to the table to engage in your personal transformation.

There will be days when you'll feel like it and days when you won't. Many times we disqualify ourselves from coming to the table because of pride, insecurity, weariness, lack, apathy, fear of failure, or a host of other hurdles. Before you go any further in this book, you have to decide that you're worth the journey. Even if you don't feel like it, you just need to keep showing up—keep coming to the table. Too often we dream about life in the palace but are unwilling to walk out of our prisons. We are deceived into thinking it will be embarrassing to admit our flaws. Pride will continue to torture us in captivity until we lay it down and humble ourselves before God, admitting that we need Him.

In light of this truth, ask yourself, "Do I really want to be free, or do I just like the idea of freedom? Am I willing to do what it takes to get free, or do I want someone else to do the work for me?"

We all desire freedom, but it's often more complex than a simple yes or no answer. Freedom means something very different to each of us, depending on the landscape and shaping of our lives. How was your relationship with your mother and father? Were they both around? What about siblings? Did you experience abuse or trauma growing up? Shame? Fear? Anger? Discontentment? Anxiety? What about walking through dark seasons that have stuck to you like they still own you? Broken relationships? Loss? Pain? The sad reality is that everyone can identify with something on this list, however incomplete it may be. As we each look back on our lives, even if we had two loving parents, a white picket fence, and a healthy church environment, the enemy has still tried to weave a tangled web of lies to keep us in bondage and isolate us. The good news is that our God has given each of us a way out of that bondage. The question is, do we actually want to partner with God to do what is necessary to live free? Or are we content with putting on a show for the rest of our lives? It's up to us.

There is no question that God wants you to live a free life, but He respects your free will enough to allow you to choose. There is always more ground to take, and once the ground is taken, it's time to pour it out and give it away to others so that they may attain the measure of freedom that God has stored up for them as well. As freedom germinates, grows, and blossoms in your life, by its very nature it must bear fruit and reproduce. You will begin to transform the culture around you.

As you prepare your heart to dive further into this book, read the following passage, marinate in it, and meditate on it. Pull it apart, talk to God about it, wrestle with it, and become it.

> It is absolutely clear that God has called you to a free life. Just make sure that you don't use this freedom as an excuse to do whatever you want to do and destroy your freedom. Rather, use your freedom to serve one another in love; that's how freedom grows. For everything we know about God's Word is summed up in a single sentence: Love others as you love yourself. That's an act of true freedom. (Gal. 5:13–14 Message)

I encourage you to read the full passage of Galatians 5:13–21 in your own time. Consider reading the entire book of Galatians in context. Let it search your heart and motives on your quest to walk in the fullness of your freedom. Let it be like a mirror that you look into. What do you see? What do you feel? How does this passage or book change you from the inside out?

Your Journey Out of Prison to Freedom

Are you ready to take responsibility for your freedom and go on the journey to get there, no matter what it looks like? A lot of times we are waiting for "someday when . . ." But someday is now. We have to choose to be proactive today and every day after that.

I remember a time when we were sitting and having a meal with Steve and Sharon Kelly, two amazing mentors and friends who serve as pastors of Wave Church in Virginia Beach. As we conversed over grilled salmon, I poured out my heart about a project I had coming up, including all of the insecurities that it had exposed in me. After I was done verbally processing all my emotions and fears, Steve looked me in the eyes with great intensity and asked, "Andi, how old are you?"

To which I replied, "Thirty-five. Why do you ask?"

"So when are you going to grow up?"

His reply hit me square between the eyes. "Well ouch . . . and thank you."

I had allowed fear and insecurity to rule my thoughts, actions, and confidence. I found it hard to take myself seriously or even back myself. I had gotten in my own way and saw myself as less than everyone else around me. Comparison truly is a killer.

A few months later, my husband made a similar observation. "It's like you're a sheriff, and you've willingly handed over your badge and weapons. It's time to take them back and step into your authority." He started to pray over me, and as he did I felt God say to me in all my inadequacy and insecurity, "I have confidence in you." The floodgates of trust in my God and His love for me were reopened where they had been shut off. To hear those words from my Father and Creator even when I didn't have confidence in myself deeply changed me.

You see, He has confidence in you even when you don't. Your inadequacy, fear, insecurity, pain, or rejection does not faze Him! Jesus died willingly in order to connect with you, to step into those moments, look you in the eyes, and say, "You've got this, because I've got you."

The steady and true encouragements from Steve and my husband brought me to a turning point. It's as if I was waiting for someone to give me permission to live free and step into my identity and destiny. God did that on the cross; what was I waiting for? What are you waiting for?

It is important to be aware that our days in this life are numbered; take each breath with gratitude and do not waste a single moment. "Teach us to number our days, that we may gain a heart of wisdom" (Ps. 90:12).

It's time to stop waiting for "someday when." Stop waiting for permission. Live the life you've only dreamed about because your time is now. Dream *with* God and run with Him. Back yourself. God has confidence in you because He is holding you. The world needs who you are, a valuable piece of a beautiful picture God is painting throughout time. History is His story, and you have been written into it. What will your chapters look like?

If you're ready to get your hands dirty, then roll up your sleeves, get on your knees, and let the tears flow until you find yourself safe in the arms of the healer. Your freedom beckons. We're in this together!

▲ ◄ ◄ Walking in Freedom ► ► ▲

1. Do you believe you are worth the investment in yourself to live free? Do you believe that the journey from the prison of lies you've lived in to the palace of truth at the table with your loving Father is yours for the taking and worth the journey? Be honest with yourself. You're going to need the bravery and wherewithal to stare your pain in the face, hold hands with the healer, and wrap yourself in His love and freedom.

2. Write a list of old mindsets you want to transform in partnership with the healer. Write what you believe you will be set free from on this journey. Keep your vision and goals before you as you go. You'll be amazed to see just what God does by the end of this book.

3. Read this prayer out loud as a declaration of faith:

> *Father, I thank You that You are present at all times whether I can feel You or not. I thank You that You made a way for me to live free by Your Son's precious sacrifice. Holy Spirit, I ask You to lead and guide me into all truth. I ask for a heightened awareness of Your whisper and leading as we connect on the journey. Jesus, I thank You for exchanging Your life for mine so that I could run into the Father's arms. Fill me with the*

deep revelation that You are within me and that my life is infused with Yours, that there is nothing that is impossible with You. Father, I ask You to send angels on assignment for protection along the journey, especially for the times when I stare my pain in the face. I know that You are with me and Your love heals me, because You are the very being of love. I ask for a deeper revelation of Your love and truth. Thank You for all that You have done, are doing, and are about to do in my life. In Jesus's name, amen.

4

Freedom from Unforgiveness

And forgive us our debts, as we also have forgiven our debtors.

Matthew 6:12

Lie: I am a better judge than God and will only forgive people when I *feel* like it.

I will always remember the day my perfect little world was disrupted by the truth of our family's painful past. I was sitting at a little boutique café in Spokane, Washington, across from my mom just months after I had given my life to Jesus at nineteen. The fire was crackling and my double-short latte was absolute sipping perfection. We were bantering back and forth about life until I felt a nudge to ask some pointed questions about my upbringing. There were some things that seemed a bit fuzzy that I wanted clarity on. Now that I had found freedom in Christ, I was ravenous for more and couldn't help but ask questions, many of which would lead me to roads that would be harder to travel down than I could have known.

As I dug deeper and deeper into the pit of darkness that my mom had prayed none of her children would ever discover, I could see her uncomfortably shifting back and forth in her seat, brow furrowed and mouth dry, visibly exuding anxiety and fear. I had hit a nerve, and apparently it was a big one. It was a nerve that I was intent on touching until I got all the information I wanted.

The knowledge of my mother and father's past laid siege to my apparently fragile emotional stability and newfound faith. When the veil was lifted, my broken heart was exposed. Looking back on that moment in time, I see a young girl in shock, protecting her heart with anger, hatred, and vengeance as she assaulted her mother with words intended to wound. In just a few minutes of conversation, she had become an object of disgust and disdain as I stepped into the role of judge and jury. The secrets she revealed with fear and trembling, knowing well that I might reject her forever, helped make sense of some of the fuzzy memories I'd had while growing up. But at the same time, they incited a deep anger that I had been keeping at bay within me. It was now exposed for all to see.

I got up from the table, shouting expletives in impassioned tones and generally making a horrific scene. I told her that I hated her and would never forgive her as I made my dramatic exit. She followed me out the door, crying and asking for forgiveness, which I refused to give. I will never forget the sight of her standing at the back door of the coffee shop as I ran to my car, pure white snow falling to rest on her shoulders as she wept, begging me not to walk away from her. She was truly repentant for her actions, but my pain and anger blinded me, cutting off all compassion in my heart. I felt that she must pay for it as long as I saw fit. I had ammunition, my mouth was the gun, and she was my target; I got good at target practice. I knew how to craft my words to cut straight to her heart, wounding her with reminders of her shameful past over and over again.

A couple of weeks after our heated conversation, I was lying on the couch reading a book when my mom walked into the kitchen. I made a point to glare at her with disdain. She paused and said something that changed my life, although she wouldn't know it for seven more years when I would give birth to my first son.

"Andi, I only hope you can forgive me one day like I know Jesus has forgiven me."

I lay there acting as though her words didn't affect me, but deep down I knew she was right. I made a conscious choice to hold on to unforgiveness, which turned into bitterness, offense, and resentment. Over the next seven years, our relationship became tolerable, but I kept my mother emotionally distant. She was no longer safe; trust had been broken.

Finding Truth

Fast-forward seven years. Since the day in the coffee shop, I had moved to Australia, completed Bible college, and married my husband. I was now as far away from my mom geographically as I had been emotionally. This distance was fine with me until I became pregnant with our first child. All of a sudden, I had a newfound sense of responsibility to deal with my issues. I knew that if I didn't work toward healing the relationship with my mom, I would pass this dysfunction on to my son, allowing it to carry on to the next generation of our family.

I had been in weekly counseling for the six months prior to my pregnancy. Many of the issues from my past had been rearing their ugly head and affecting not only my marriage but also my ability to lead in church and function in life. I was getting the help I needed in that particular season to get free. Each week there was some sort of breakthrough, as God gently revealed things and healed me along the way.

Becoming pregnant opened up the "mom" jar, and it was time to go there. I was about to become a mother myself, which caused me to think about all the cruel ways I had been treating my own mom. I realized that if my kids treated me the way I was treating her, I would be heartbroken. Yet the truth still remained that my mom had deeply hurt me, and I needed healing from the pain.

Paul and I went away to Dunk Island for our "baby moon" about a month before Ezekiel arrived. My counseling had focused on my past abuse and sexual sin, so a friend recommended that I read the book *Kissed the Girls and Made Them Cry* by Lisa Bevere. Little did I know that this book would equip me for the breakthrough with my mom that was right around the corner.

Paul had gone out to the beach to relax, and I stayed back in the room because I was feeling very large and pregnant and way too tired to move. I grabbed the book and settled into bed to read. As I read the biblical story of the adulterous woman "caught in the very act" and thrown at the feet of the Pharisees, Lisa's compelling storytelling captured my heart and brought me to a place of repentance and forgiveness. As I bring you into a moment that began a restoration journey between my mother and me, allow me to paint the picture of grace and forgiveness in John 8 with my own words.

The mouths of the accusers froth for justice as they violently throw the woman to Jesus's feet. She is an adulterer, caught in the very act—naked, broken, disheveled, humiliated, and full of shame before a crowd of onlooking religious zealots. Jesus looks down at her as she writhes in pain, grabbing at her open wounds from the brutal and very public journey to the temple, the "holy" Pharisees dragging her naked body over hard rock and coarse sand through winding streets. As Jesus gazes into her eyes, the crowd holds their breath with expectancy for justice to be had. The law is clear: she should die.

Instead, his eyes turn away as he kneels down, staring at the temple floor. His hands extend, tracing words on the ground that, to this day, not a soul knows. Is he stalling? Is he sending a message? Is he listening to his Father for direction? Is he drawing a line in the sand?

The Pharisees, spitting with anger, yell demands for judgment, testing him in front of the crowds. "What do you say we should do, Jesus?!"

Jesus stands up slowly, looking into the woman's questioning eyes with kindness and understanding. Her soul is met with a dignity that every living person desires. He turns to the Pharisees, and with wisdom that could only pour down from His Father in heaven, says to them, "He who is without sin among you, let him be the first to cast a stone at her." The resulting silence is palpable as Jesus again lowers himself to draw. There is no response from the men, only a breeze weaving through the streets, whistling gently against buildings.

In one sentence, Jesus disqualified each man and woman present from the seat of judgment, while, unknown to them, simultaneously qualifying himself, the sinless Lamb. The stark reminder of their own law permits no response; not one of them is without sin, and they know it. As each Pharisee walks out in sequence, the crowd thins until only a few onlookers remain; without condemnation, what fun is to be had?

Jesus looks again with dignity and forgiveness at the woman, who is still wrapped in thoughts of her compromising lifestyle and shame, now on public display. "Woman, where are they? Has no one condemned you?"

She raises her head, wincing, wondering if a stone is already on its path to her broken flesh. Instead, the piercing eyes of Jesus confront her heart with a purity she has never experienced: love. Does his kindness not come with a price? To her own surprise, she replies, "No one, sir."

The only One worthy of the judgment seat remains in front of her. His words of forgiveness release a grace through love that overwhelms her heart. "Then neither do I condemn you. Now go and leave your life of sin."

She is forever changed!

This story took me back to that moment when I lay on the couch, glaring at my mom while she prayed I would one day be able to forgive her like she knew Jesus had forgiven her. I wept, recalling my cruelty and bitter unforgiveness.

Alone in that room, except for the child in my womb, I cried out, "Oh, God! Oh God! I forgive my mom! I forgive her! You have loved her always, and I do too! I forgive her!"

Right after those deep, penitent words came out of my mouth, it was as if Jesus himself entered the room next to me, and I heard His response ring in my ears, "That's so good, sweetheart, because you were the Pharisee that threw her at my feet, when you should have been on the ground next to her, on your knees, asking for forgiveness."

I dropped to the ground with my eight-month-pregnant belly protruding against my thighs and wept, repenting and asking for forgiveness—forgiveness for the judgment I had held against my mom when it was never my seat to sit in. The judgment seat has room for only One, and it doesn't have a name tag on it reading "Andi Andrew."

Are You a Pharisee?

The following verse is sobering: "For we must all appear before the judgment seat of Christ, so that each of us may receive what is due us for the things done while in the body, whether good or bad" (2 Cor. 5:10). When we are confronted with our pharisaical ways, do we walk away or remain with Jesus until his love softens the most calloused part of our hearts? We have all stood in the place of a self-righteous Pharisee, believing our ways and thoughts are right, not wanting to forgive and desiring payment for another's sins. We have all thrown people at the feet of Jesus, acting as though we stand holy in our own works, when the only one who makes us holy stands before us. We need to get on the ground, suck some dirt, repent, turn from our judgment, and forgive others. Forgiveness precipitates a beautiful process of redemption and reconciliation.

I've heard it said that unforgiveness is like drinking poison and expecting someone else to die. It's true. I know that when I hold on to unforgiveness, I become bitter and deeply offended, and a little piece of my heart hardens to intimacy with God. Wounding has this effect; it causes us to self-preserve instead of letting the healer in.

It's good to live with a healthy awareness of the real judge; it's not us. We all fall short in this area, judging others or ourselves without even thinking twice, as Christ taps us on the shoulder and asks if He can have His seat back.

Don't pick on people, jump on their failures, criticize their faults—unless, of course, you want the same treatment. That critical spirit has a way of boomeranging. It's easy to see a smudge on your neighbor's face and be oblivious to the ugly sneer on your own. Do you have the nerve to say, "Let me wash your face for you," when your own face is distorted by contempt? It's this whole traveling road-show mentality all over again, playing a holier-than-thou part instead of just living your part. Wipe that ugly sneer off your own face, and you might be fit to offer a washcloth to your neighbor. (Matt. 7:1–5 Message)

I don't know about you, but most of the time, we want to forgive when we feel like it. But who ever *feels* like forgiving someone? Forgiveness is much more than a feeling; it is an intentional lifestyle choice and a command from Jesus himself: "Forgive us our debts, as we also have forgiven our debtors" (Matt. 6:12).

The Lord's Prayer is Jesus's instruction on how to pray, and He clearly sees forgiving those who owe us a debt as a priority, intended to be part of our daily prayer life. Yet we are often waiting for the perfect moment, when it *feels* right. We want to *feel* the ability to forgive well up in our hearts and take over our will. Unfortunately, it doesn't always work that way.

Forgiveness Quota

As we choose to release others' debts and thus free ourselves from the captivity of unforgiveness, we're hoping that we'll never *think* of these individuals again. But the reality is, they are likely part of our everyday lives, which gives us an opportunity on a daily basis for a heart check. When I see them, how does my heart respond? Do I still have a pang of anxiety in my stomach when I spot them in a crowd? Does adrenaline still shoot through my body? Do I still feel like wrestling them to the ground and pounding them furiously with my fists? Oh, wait—or is that just me?

Forgiveness is simply a choice made of our free will that we engage in time and time again. It is an essential key to freedom that we cannot ignore. We have the power to be released from our personal prisons—you know, the prisons we find ourselves in screaming at the top of our lungs for someone to release us from our bondage, as the Holy Spirit softly whispers to us, "You hold the key in your hands to let yourself out, and that key is forgiveness."

I have lost track of the number of times I've had to forgive, and I will continue to forgive countless more times until the day I die. Matthew 18:21–22 says, "Then Peter came to

Jesus and asked, 'Lord, how many times shall I forgive my brother or sister who sins against me? Up to seven times?' Jesus answered, 'I tell you, not seven times, but seventy-seven times.'" I love that Peter is trying to meet a minimum number of times that he *has to* forgive. His mindset is still rooted in Hebrew law, while Jesus is displaying a "more excellent way"—love, which satisfies all godly laws. Jesus hadn't yet died and resurrected, yet everything He taught and demonstrated pointed to the New Covenant to come. It's fair to assume that a question like this probably wasn't out of the ordinary. Yet if we live like this on the other side of the cross, wondering what the "forgiveness quota" of the day is, then all we're doing is checking all the boxes while placing ourselves back under the law, toiling for our freedom. The New Covenant is all about the state of our heart.

Jesus's answer, when interpreted through a Hebrew background, actually seems impossible, because it means *every* time, or *infinity* times. There goes Peter's plans of being a certified "good boy." A life of radical forgiveness—one that attains to Jesus's—is not possible without the grace and forgiveness of God in our own lives.

Life will always present us with moments when we have a simple choice between forgiveness and condemnation. If we choose forgiveness, we will remain in love and freedom. If we choose to condemn and hold others' debts against them, we subject ourselves to captivity and bitterness.

Reconciliation

I am so glad I had that moment on the floor in Dunk Island, because the next month I gave birth to my first son.

I desperately wanted him to come into the world with the cleanest slate I could give him as a mom with a little less baggage than before. I was also keenly aware that my mother was flying out for a whole month to stay with us. Having her in such close proximity was going to present countless opportunities for forgiveness and healing.

I have a vivid memory of the day she arrived. The two of us were sitting on the floor in Zeke's room just days before he entered the world. The morning sun was streaming through the windows, warming our backs, as we folded his tiny, recently purchased clothes. I was asking questions about what labor was going to be like, and my mom was giving advice on what to do and what not to do. As she finished speaking, there was a moment of silence. I paused, knowing what was coming, and slowly opened my mouth. Trapped in my heart for too long, the words poured out like a flood.

"Mom. I'm sorry. I'm so sorry that the last seven years I have hurt you and made you pay for the sins of your past. I'm sorry that I've held such judgment and disdain for you, making sure that you felt every bit of it. I'm sorry that I made you feel like you're the only one who has sinned in this world. I'm sorry that I have been so self-righteous, acting as though I'm perfect when I now know so deeply that I'm not."

I went on to tell her about my experience reading the story of the adulterous woman, receiving a revelation and acknowledgment of my pharisaical ways, and how it changed me. After I recounted the story, I asked, "I have forgiven you just as Jesus has. Now will you forgive me?"

By this stage we were both crying, hearts fully laid bare. She looked me in the eyes, tears spilling down her cheeks, and simply said, "Yes." I don't know how long we held each other on the floor, covered in Ezekiel's scattered baby clothes, while the sun shone down on us like a smile from heaven. It was an embrace that brought a healing salve of redemption and restoration. We were put back together—reconciled—not as we once were, but as we were always meant to be.

I can't say that after that moment everything was perfect. It was as though we both had willingly invested in a renovator's dream fixer-upper house. We gave all that we had to buy it, knowing full well that it would take a lot of work to make it reach its final beauty. In that moment, we both committed to the journey together, to do whatever was required to restore our trust and intimacy. It is a journey we are still on to this day.

Forgiveness Is a Constant Choice

Immediately after Jesus told Peter to live a life of constant forgiveness, he illustrates what failing to do so looks like in the parable of the unmerciful servant.

> The kingdom of heaven is like a king who wanted to settle accounts with his servants. As he began the settlement, a man who owed him ten thousand bags of gold was brought to him. Since he was not able to pay, the master ordered that he and his wife and his children and all that he had be sold to repay the debt. At this the servant fell on his knees before him. "Be patient with me," he begged, "and I will pay back everything." The servant's master took pity on him, canceled the debt and let him go. But when that servant went out, he found one of his fellow servants who owed him a hundred silver coins. He grabbed him and began to choke him. "Pay

back what you owe me!" he demanded. His fellow servant fell to his knees and begged him, "Be patient with me, and I will pay it back." But he refused. Instead, he went off and had the man thrown into prison until he could pay the debt. When the other servants saw what had happened, they were outraged and went and told their master everything that had happened. Then the master called the servant in. "You wicked servant," he said, "I canceled all that debt of yours because you begged me to. Shouldn't you have had mercy on your fellow servant just as I had on you?" In anger his master handed him over to the jailers to be tortured, until he should pay back all he owed. "This is how my heavenly Father will treat each of you unless you forgive your brother or sister from your heart." (Matt. 18:23–35)

Remember how I said earlier: "Judgment seat, party of one"? The unmerciful servant *did* get the memo, but he chose to sit in the seat that wasn't his anyway.

Just like the unmerciful servant, we beg for the forgiveness of our own sin and shame, and it's freely given to us because it was paid for on the cross. But when we are asked to engage that same level of forgiveness with others, we go out and "spiritually" choke anyone who owes us a debt. We want them to apologize for what they did, to write us a letter that demeans themselves, ensuring that we feel better in their wallowing. We daydream twisted visions of our debtors making public addresses of repentance to appease our bruised ego.

You may feel, even now, as though you are in a spiritual prison—tormented and tortured. Whom do you need to forgive to release yourself? You may even need to forgive yourself, intentionally doing away with what seems like perpetual self-hatred that has kept you from allowing God's love to heal your heart. You will be amazed at the freedom you find as you forgive those who have hurt you. Remember, forgiveness isn't a magical potion. It's an act of our free will that begins a process of healing, reconciliation, and freedom in our lives; we may not feel it immediately.

I don't know what you've been through or who you need to forgive, but forgiving is necessary for our freedom and a natural overflow of the grace, love, and forgiveness that have been extended to us. Ephesians 4:32 says, "Be kind to one another, tenderhearted, forgiving one another, just as God in Christ forgave you" (ESV). *The Gospel-Centered Life* puts it this way:

> Scripture assumes that if we have truly experienced God's forgiveness in the gospel, we will be radically forgiving towards others. By contrast, if we are unforgiving, resentful, or bitter toward others, it's a sure sign that we are not living out of the deep joy and freedom of the gospel. Our forgiveness of others is intended to mirror the forgiveness God has given us.[1]

You don't have to, but you will be forgiven as you forgive others, so it's probably a good idea to forgive even if you don't feel like it. Remember Matthew 18:35: "This is how my heavenly Father will treat each of you unless you forgive your brother or sister from your heart." Ouch. Now that's some truth with a big love stick that we all need to be hit with from time to time. Notice it says from your heart, not simply with your mouth. Forgiveness is a matter of the heart; Jesus came to deal with the root of our problems, not just the symptoms. He came for a revolution in our hearts and consequently our entire lives.

New Life

The month that followed Zeke's birth was glorious and full of redemptive moments between my mom and me: conversations, prayer, arguments, wrestling with the truth, and sheer joy when my firstborn son entered the world.

Zeke was born after eight hours of intense labor. We had burned some CDs (yes, we still used those at the time) of my favorite worship songs and jokingly called them "Birth's Greatest Hits," with the goal of bringing the presence of God into my labor. I don't think it was a coincidence that Ezekiel Benjamin Andrew (which means "God makes strong" and "the son of my right hand") was born to the anthem, "Our God Is an Awesome God." It was a glorious moment full of laughter and relief when he entered into the world.

When I looked down to see him, his body was blue and limp, and I knew instinctively that something was wrong. Just seconds after he was laid on my chest to bond, the midwives ripped him away in great haste to resuscitate him. Doctors, midwives, and nurses flooded into the room to care for him. We found out later that he was what was known as a "flat baby," grunting desperately to breathe.

He was rushed off to the NICU and after a few hours of fervent and effective prayer from family and friends, he miraculously turned around. The midwife on call brought him into the room because he was hungry and hadn't had his first feeding. The moment they put him in my arms, he looked up at me with his piercing, deep-brownish-blue eyes and held his gaze. I sobbed with joy and delight. My son had come into the world and was given a momma who knew how to forgive! I was proud of myself in that moment. I wasn't perfect, but I had done my best to pave a way for my son to walk in footsteps that looked a little more like Jesus. I bonded with my son and didn't ever want to let him go.

Lying there with my freshly born baby boy, I pored over the last seven years with my mom in my head and heart and was suddenly able to relate more deeply and personally. Would I want my kids to treat me the way I treated her for the last seven years? No! Do I hope they will forgive me for all the blunders I am yet to make as an imperfect mother? Yes! Again, I repented and then prayed for the relationships I was to forge with my own children—the one in my arms and the little ones to come: "Oh God, may they be filled deeply with your great love. May they know how to forgive much because they are forgiven much. May they know repentance and the joy of walking in your restorative power!"

Then it hit me: Zeke's date of birth, July 31, 2005, after eight hours of labor, was exactly eight years to the day that I gave my life to Jesus in Spokane, Washington—the day that Jesus made all things new in me. Now, exactly eight years later in Sydney, Australia, God was making all things new between my mom and me as I birthed the next generation of our family. In fact, the Hebraic meaning for the number eight in the Bible represents a new beginning. All things had been made new as a new generation was birthed on the earth.

Trust the Kingdom Process

Neither your past pain nor your current season defines who you are. Yet you do have to face your hurts, without fear, and give them to Jesus the healer, not shying away from those gritty moments in your current season. The Father's love for you defines who you are.

So much shame and isolation can come from abuse, betrayal, and pain. If the enemy can get you to buy into lies such as "you're just like this," or "you can't be loved like this," he can slowly convince you to hand your destiny over to him. While it can take time to unravel and rewire our lives after experiencing tragedy, abuse, or betrayal, I'm here to tell you that freedom is along the whole journey, no matter what the speed!

So what do we do when our past has shaped who we are today? We know that our upbringing, surroundings, and experiences have influenced us, but Jesus paid for us to be *un*influenced by these things. Jesus came so that we could live our lives in and through Him, not our past pain or experience. Coming to a point of maturity in our walk with God is where we begin to walk through the kingdom process, which is the antithesis of the worldly process—blame, revenge, judgment, hatred, offense, and bitterness.

The story of Michelangelo's statue of David, one of the most iconic statues in the world, beautifully illustrates the way our God sculpts our very lives into reflections of His glory using the kingdom process.

The statue of David was originally commissioned to be sculpted by an artist named Agostino. He only got as far as shaping the legs, feet, and torso, and then for unknown reasons the project was halted for ten years. It was then picked up by another artist, Antonio Rossellino, who soon after starting the project dropped it for reasons still unknown. The massive piece of costly marble was then left in the yard of the cathedral workshop, abandoned and exposed to the elements for twenty-five years!

At this point, some of you may be *feeling* as though you have been neglected by Father God in the process of becoming who He created you to be. Maybe you started following Jesus, the work began, but things have happened to you that brought lingering pain into your heart. Maybe your pain has grown into bitterness because you've allowed offense and unforgiveness to flourish. The condition of your heart has in turn caused you to feel neglected, abandoned "outside" to be battered by the elements. The story isn't over yet.

There began to be concern for this costly piece of marble, which barely resembled its intended figure, left lying on its back in the cathedral yard. It had been thrown aside and ignored; yet it still possessed every bit as much potential as it ever did. Those who discovered it during an inventory of the cathedral yard were determined to find a truly great artist who could take this neglected yet costly block of marble and shape it into a masterpiece that would be admired for generations to come. In steps master craftsman Michelangelo who, at a mere twenty-six years old, convinced the council to give him the commission.

Our God is the true master artist, who can take the most broken-down, bitter, shameful life and turn it into a work of art that brings glory to His name. The statue of David is one of Michelangelo's great achievements. His genius is glorified in his work of art just as God's genius is glorified in our restoration. When people look at the masterpiece of our lives, forged out of the kingdom process, our Creator's name will inevitably come to mind. They will see that He took what was impossibly hard, unwieldy, and neglected and chiseled it into something beautiful: the image of God.

Michelangelo is sometimes credited with saying: "In every block of marble I see a statue as plain as though it stood before me, shaped and perfect in attitude and action. I have only to hew away the rough walls that imprison the lovely apparition to reveal it to the other eyes as mine see it."[2]

That's what God sees when he looks at us! When we forgive, we allow the artist to begin to chisel away the pain in our lives. In the hands of the artist, we are shaped and sculpted into everything we were meant to be and placed back in society right where we belong. We were made to be a masterpiece! Our deliverance and freedom are found in the chipping away process. This truth is solidified for us in Philippians 1:6: "Being confident of this, that he who began a good work in you will carry it on to completion until the day of Christ Jesus."

Making It Practical

So now what? By this point, you've probably identified several people you need to forgive. Maybe you need to ask God for forgiveness or even forgive yourself to get started. How do you do it? You don't need to wait to go to church and go forward on a "forgiveness" altar call to do so. You can pray a simple prayer like the one below anytime it's needed. Put it in your phone, save it to your computer, print it out and keep it in your wallet, memorize it, whatever it takes—but use it!

Lord, today as an act of my will I choose to forgive _____ for hurting me. Specifically, I forgive them for _____.

*I choose to release them from their sin against me;
I cancel the debt they owe me, and I release them into
Your hands. I release them from any judgment or criti-
cism that I have held against them, and I trust You to
deal with the situation and memory as You see fit. I
understand that they have issues, and they are not mine
to carry or fix.*

*In the name of Jesus and by the power of His blood,
I ask that He seal this heavenly transaction. And by the
power of Jesus's blood, I cancel Satan's authority over
me in this situation and in this memory.*

*God, I ask that You forgive me for sitting in the judg-
ment seat and taking Your place of authority in trying
to execute justice. I thank You that You forgive me liber-
ally and completely, and I choose to exercise the same
forgiveness to those who owe me a debt they cannot pay.*

Keep this prayer in your heart, because you'll need it for
the rest of your life. Don't wait until you feel like forgiving;
you never will. It's an act of your will that carries a grace to
change you, whether you feel it or not.

Follow Jesus's Example

Sometimes we act as though Jesus is out of touch with our
humanity. We treat Him as a Bible character when, in fact,
He was and is our real, living, breathing Savior who put skin
on and walked a mile in our shoes.

Sweat poured out, dripping like blood down onto the harsh
and unforgiving ground in the Garden of Gethsemane right
before He gave His life to rescue us all. He asked His Father

if there could be another way, yet He laid down His will and went to the cross anyway.

Judas betrayed Jesus unto death, one of His, the men He consciously chose to invest all He had into. He could have called down legions of angels to have vengeance against this "friend" and disciple, yet He went to the cross anyway.

On the very night of His betrayal, He washed the feet of those who would betray and deny Him. And He went to the cross anyway—for His accusers and betrayers.

In Jesus's darkest hour of need, Peter, one of His closest friends, ran away in fear. Peter had professed very publicly that he would never leave Him, yet when all was on the line, he abandoned Jesus, and Jesus went to the cross anyway.

He was falsely accused and publicly humiliated. He was mocked, abused, and made a spectacle of. He didn't answer back in anger, shame, or pride. He went to the cross anyway, even for all of His abusers.

When Jesus was on the cross suffering, He didn't quit or question the mission. He submitted himself to the heavenly plan . . . and He stayed on the cross and gave up His life—for you, for me, for all.

What do you do when those you invest into or trust betray you? What do you do when your closest friends abandon you in your time of greatest need because they don't know what to say or do with you? What do you do when someone you trust abuses you and breaks that trust? What do you do when the church you're a part of is imperfect (as they all are) and causes you pain and to question things? What do you do when the family that was supposed to cover and protect you abandons you? What do you do when you're afraid to let go and forgive because it may all spiral out of control?

I urge you to follow Jesus's example and go to the cross anyway. Even if you don't want to, even if you feel justified in your pain and anger. You are free to ask the Father if there is another way—He can take it. I'm here to tell you from experience and years of pain and questioning: the cross is the only way. Go there daily. Go there and forgive those who have trespassed against you, just as you have trespassed against the Father who sent His One and Only Son to that cross to release you from the torment you have been living in.

The choice is yours. Go to the cross. Freedom is available to you, but you have to move.

Truth: Forgiveness releases me from the prison I find myself in. I may or may not feel like forgiving, but as I choose to engage my free will, true forgiveness from my heart has the power to set me free.

▲ ◄ ◄ Walking in Freedom ► ► ▲

1. Get into a quiet space that is familiar and safe for you. Ask the Holy Spirit whether there is anything you need to ask forgiveness for. Lay it before Jesus, and receive the fullness of the forgiveness that is yours.

2. Now ask God if there is anyone you need to forgive. If yes, place the person or people you need to forgive before Jesus. They're probably the people who have popped up in your heart as you have read this chapter. Invite the Holy Spirit to soften your heart as you prepare to release yourself from the prison of unforgiveness.

3. Pray the forgiveness prayer provided in this chapter out loud for each person individually. If it's a group of people you're forgiving, mention the group. Remember, forgiveness is the beginning of the process. You may or may not feel anything, but truth supersedes your feelings! Your prayer is a heavenly transaction that frees you from your personal prison. If you'd like to have someone you trust with you as you pray, that's fine.

4. Take a moment and ask if you need to forgive yourself for anything. We often forget how easily we condemn and judge ourselves because we feel we deserve it.

5. Repeat as necessary for the rest of your life.

5

Freedom from Fear

I prayed to the Lord, and he answered me. He freed me from all my fears.

Psalm 34:4 NLT

Lie: Fear has permission to rob me of my vision and destiny.

New Year's Eve 2015 was awesome. Surrounded by my kiddos and good friends, wearing comfy clothes and no makeup, and watching the Disney Channel, I celebrated the coming of 2016 with joy. But the first day of the new year? No bueno. Inadequate, anxious, and fearful are not the sort of words or resolutions that one writes down to "walk in" for the upcoming year. While fear wasn't my plan for 2016, it was staring me in the face on day one.

I often feel inadequate when embarking on something new, which can be an indicator of what's going on in my heart (Prov. 4:23). Whenever I feel totally out of my depth, unable to achieve what I am supposed to do, I know I've stepped out of connection with God and have started to walk in striving and fear. Our Father never asked us to perform for Him to either earn His love or prove ours, yet sometimes we act like He has.

As evening approached on January 1st, we began our drive home to Brooklyn from our friends' house on Long Island. Not long into the drive I started having multiple heart palpitations that literally took my breath away. I had been having them for a few months prior here and there, but these were one on top of another. Fear began to creep in because of the palpitations, paired with deep worries of inadequacy for the year ahead. The pressures of life, some of which are burdens we put on ourselves, were beginning to accumulate: speaking engagements booked for the year, deadlines for my first book (the one that you're reading), loving and leading my children well, building an even better marriage, and pastoring a growing church with love, truth, wisdom, and strength. All of these commitments felt like weights on my shoulders, laid there by self-imposed expectations that were unrealistic and motivated in performance. The pressure was causing me to crumble, and my body was manifesting what was going on in my spirit.

With each heart palpitation, I actually began to picture myself dying. I imagined that they were a sign of heart disease and that I was going to have a cardiac arrest and die young. I even pictured my children without their mother and wondered whom Paul would marry when I was gone. As I started to tear up, picturing my impending death, the grip of irrational fear on my heart was complete. It's amazing how quickly we can agree to ride down such scary, dangerous, and entirely false roads of thinking.

As we drove home, the sun was gently fading, peacefully eclipsed behind clouds with shooting rays of golden light and hues of pink, purple, and orange swirling together, and beckoning me to lay my burdens down and rest as evening approached. Paul asked me what was wrong, and I poured out my deepest fears. He grabbed my hand and held it tightly, assuring me his love was near with every squeeze and silent nod. We put on worship music, and as one of our sons in the backseat began to sing out so sweetly, we both started to cry.

The truth is, six months prior to that moment, I had started to feel my heart disconnect from feeling anything, causing the familiar, lingering of depression to come knocking on my door. This was a particularly strange phenomenon for me, because I'm very much a "feeler," and have been as long as I can remember. I used to believe it was a weakness, until I realized God is happy about the way He made me. I feel the atmosphere of a room when I walk into it, the mood and temperament of people I encounter, and the emotions of joy and pain in the deepest places of my soul. So when my feelings began to shut down and numbness set in, I knew something was very wrong. I felt myself shift into self-preservation mode, refusing to trust anyone around me. I even began to shut God out as I surrounded my heart with worries, fears, and inadequacies that served as insulation from intimacy and disappointment.

Later that evening, we dropped off our kiddos with our incredible life assistant for the evening. Paul and I left for Manhattan to go out to dinner with two good friends who had arrived in the city at the outset of the year to invest into our worship team and speak at our church communities the first Sunday of the year.

As we hung out and caught up on our lives since we had last met, our conversation led me to pour out my struggling, fearful heart. I talked about my feelings of inadequacy for the year ahead and the pain that the year prior had brought. Seeing the love in their eyes for me, containing no judgment or agenda, was like looking into the eyes of Jesus. My husband squeezed my hand (lots of hand squeezing that day) and nodded in agreement with a big smile. He too adored me right where I was. The love from these three people was almost too much to receive but it was a love that was chasing my fears away.

When I was honest and vulnerable with people I trusted, even in the midst of my inadequacy, it brought about a moment of truth and connection. As we talked, I had the opportunity to confront a lie that held me bound, and the light of truth began to shine on the darkness in me chasing my fears away. Fear is not who I am.

Isn't it true that life is a series of "do whatever it takes to be free" moments? If we pay attention, lay down our pride, and open up, we'll continue to walk in our rhythm of grace. There is still work to be done because fear is a relentless foe that knocks on the door of our hearts in countless ways. I often have to recognize it, verbally break agreement with it, and consciously partner with the truth.

The Truth about Fear

Fear is the root of anxiety, worry, control, anger, paranoia, shame, insecurity, manipulation, intimidation, unbelief, isolation, inadequacy, apathy, addiction, and people pleasing. Fear is rooted in self-preservation. When we doubt the goodness of God and the truth that death is defeated, we by necessity turn to ourselves for preservation and prosperity. All of the other mindsets mentioned—anxiety, worry, control, and so on—have to do with preserving self. Fear can even make us feel crazy or physically sick because of the destructive cycle of thinking it breeds within us.

These are some examples of lies that fear circulates in our thought life: What will people think of me? Do people think of me? What if I'm left out? Why am I always misunderstood? What if I fail? What if I disappoint my parents? What will my pastor think of me? Why am I afraid to grow up? What if change will make me feel out of control? What if I look like a fool? What if I never get married? What if I get divorced just like my parents did? What if people reject me when they find out the sort of person I am? What if I never have a baby? What if I mess my kids up just like my parents messed me up? Sometimes our thoughts go down negative spirals, as when we hear strange sounds in the middle of the night and wonder if someone is breaking in to rob us and hurt our family.

Fear is at the root of more things we face than we're probably aware of. Fear is a tool that the devil custom designs for each of our lives because it is void of the love of God. God is love (1 John 4:16), and when we fear, at our core—whether consciously or subconsciously—we're partnering with a lie that we are cut off from God's love. But we cannot be separated from God's love, as Romans 8:38–39 tells us:

> And I am convinced that nothing can ever separate us from God's love. Neither death nor life, neither angels nor demons, neither our fears for today nor our worries about tomorrow—not even the powers of hell can separate us from God's love. No power in the sky above or in the earth below—indeed, nothing in all creation will ever be able to separate us from the love of God that is revealed in Christ Jesus our Lord. (NLT)

Stopping Fear in Its Tracks

So how do we combat fear? How do we cut the ropes of worry in which we may find ourselves tangled?

Matthew 6:25–33 tells us not to worry because we are *valuable* in God's sight:

> Therefore I tell you, do not worry about your life, what you will eat or drink; or about your body, what you will wear. Is not life more than food, and the body more than clothes? Look at the birds of the air; they do not sow or reap or store away in barns, and yet your heavenly Father feeds them. Are you not much more valuable than they? Can any one of you by worrying add a single hour to your life? . . . But seek first his kingdom and his righteousness, and all these things will be given to you as well.

God's overwhelming, abundant love for us meets our every need. When we begin to recognize this and understand more of our identity and purpose in God, worry and fear begin to fall to the wayside. Worry leads to a striving life of self-preservation instead of one of rest in God's unfailing love. When we seek Him first, we are rewarded with Him; He is the prize! When we claw after our destiny in fear, we reap further anxiety and striving, and the "stuff" we accumulate must be maintained by our own strength.

If we desire freedom, then we must begin seeking what matters most: God and His kingdom. Everything else you need will be provided because your Father is good. As we build on that foundation, our fears will bow to the authority and power of Jesus in our lives.

This shift in our will is a choice; we do not have to partner with or submit to worry and fear. It will come knocking at our door, asking to be let in, but we are free to leave the door shut and shake off fear when it comes at us. We are empowered to do so by God Himself, but fear will lie and tell us that we're not. It will say that we have no authority to look it in the face and speak the truth and promise of God.

Some of the church today is crippled by the lack of revelation and understanding of the authority that it has been given in the resurrection power of Jesus Christ. The same power that raised Him from the dead is alive and at work in us (Rom. 8:11), but so often we don't understand, believe, acknowledge, or tap into it. Can you imagine what our lives would look like if we lived in that reality? Tapping into what we have access to in Christ starts with faith. I know that sounds simple, yet truly believing deep within our hearts that God can set us free from fear, even when it seems impossible, is where we begin. Faith is the *substance* of things *hoped* for and the *evidence* of things *not yet* seen! (Heb.11:1).

Substance: material, tangible physical matter, essence, something specific

Hope: expectation, confident desire, trust

Evidence: sign, proof

Maybe you lack freedom in certain areas of your life yet, but believing that it can and will happen is the evidence of your faith, bringing a confident hope and expectation that God will bring the substance of His promises into your life!

Be alert, awake, and aware that the author of lies is bent on destroying everything God is building in us: "The thief comes only to steal and kill and destroy" (John 10:10). So what must we do? "Be sober-minded; be watchful. Your adversary the devil prowls around like a roaring lion, seeking someone to devour" (1 Pet. 5:8 ESV).

The question is, will we allow the devil to devour us? Remember, it's his primary goal. But the good news is, we have all authority in Christ Jesus to resist the devil and cause him to flee as we acknowledge the love that we are never separated from. Our authority is wrapped up in Jesus and what He did for us. "Submit yourselves, then, to God. Resist the devil, and he will flee from you" (James 4:7). Notice in this verse that submission to God is what gives us authority to resist the devil. Many of us try to resist the devil while only *incorporating* Jesus into our lives. Jesus cannot be incorporated; submitting ourselves fully to Him and continuously choosing *not* to submit to fear (Matt. 6:24a) strengthens the muscle of our faith and brings about transformation.

Faith and Authority

It's also good for each of us to remember that fear only has the amount of authority that we give to it. So what is authority? One definition of authority is this: "The power or right to give orders, make decisions, and enforce obedience."[1] So does fear have the right to give you orders, or are you silencing it at its first whisper?

Faith and authority go hand in hand. In your own time, read the story of the centurion to dig deeper into this truth (Matt. 8:5–13). In short, the centurion had faith in Jesus's ability to heal his paralyzed servant. He understood that Jesus had authority to heal without even being present in the room. He understood that at Jesus's word, his servant would be healed. Jesus's authoritative words carry a heavier weight than our fear, so what are you putting your faith in? It's good to note that fear *is* a form of faith, but it's faith in the wrong kingdom.

If you were told that your father had died and left you an inheritance, wouldn't you want to read the will to find out what was left to you? Of course! Jesus died and was resurrected, leaving us a rich inheritance of life and promise, but we have to read the will to know what is ours. When we don't know what we have, it's hard to walk in authority as a daughter. Reading the Word of God causes us to know our authority and receive promises, such as the following, with open hearts:

> The LORD is my light and my salvation;
>   whom shall I fear?
> The LORD is the stronghold of my life;
>   of whom shall I be afraid? . . .

> Though an army encamp against me,
>   my heart shall not fear;
> though war arise against me,
>   yet I will be confident. (Ps. 27:1–3 ESV)

Peace I leave with you; my peace I give you. I do not give to you as the world gives. Do not let your hearts be troubled and do not be afraid. (John 14:27)

For I am convinced that neither death nor life, neither angels nor demons, neither the present nor the future, nor any powers, neither height nor depth, nor anything else in all creation, will be able to separate us from the love of God that is in Christ Jesus our Lord. (Rom. 8:38–39)

His peace and his love never leave us. We need only still ourselves and become aware of His presence in our lives. We don't have to strive for peace or love; they are the very being of our God.

Fear Is a "Familiar Spirit"

Many Christians talk about "fighting the battle" and forget that we have already won! No matter what, we fight *from* a place of victory because the battle is the Lord's. Everything we need to live in peace has been given to us, even when our worlds seem to be falling apart around us. Our circumstances do not have to be given the power to rob us of rest unless we hand our minds over. When we are set free from a spirit of fear (Eph. 6:10–12) that has been operating in our lives, don't be surprised if it comes knocking on the door of your heart trying to get back in. In some places I've heard this called a *familiar spirit*. This type is the worst kind of offender because it acts like it still has a place of authority in our lives even after we've kicked it out.

Familiar spirits are like friends we told not to come over anymore because all they do is walk in the front door, open our fridge, take whatever they want, and take advantage of our good graces. They settle in on the couch, turn on the TV, and start talking to us as if they were invited to have that place in our lives, though we've told them time and time again not to return because it's not a healthy friendship. Yet, here they are again, yapping away, trying to reclaim their place in our lives, uninvited and totally lacking boundaries. We have to get good at saying, "I told you to go, so leave and stay out." We might expect some kickback, but we don't have to accept their behavior anymore.

Once we've been set free from a spirit of fear (or any spirit) that has had authority for a long period of time in our lives, we'll have to be ready to take action against it when it tries to walk back in. Familiar spirits, and any spirit from the pit of hell, are lawless and act under the assumption that they do have a place in our lives. Once recognized, simply ignoring them doesn't make them go away. Actively breaking agreement with a familiar spirit in Jesus's name and coming into agreement with love and truth changes everything. We shouldn't let them convince us that they can stick around or hide. They can't. Jesus paid the price for our full freedom, not partial freedom, but we have to do the work to stay free—our faith is active, not passive.

Fear Is a Cage

Fear becomes a cage that we assume we're supposed to live in simply because fear is a mindset we adopt over time. But the Bible tells us there is no fear in love. So we must ask ourselves, what are we choosing to dwell in—fear or love? Psalm 91 says, "Whoever dwells in the shelter of the Most High will rest in the shadow of the Almighty. I will say of the LORD, 'He is my refuge and my fortress, my God, in whom I trust'" (vv. 1–2).

What we dwell on is what we dwell in and become, whether life-giving or death-dealing. From a place of rest in the shelter of the Most High, we have an understanding and deep revelation that we can trust Him as our only true refuge and fortress. And who is the Most High, Almighty Lord whom we love, serve, and dwell in? He is love. When we dwell in Him, we dwell in love and become love, which is always absent of fear: "There is no fear in love. But perfect love drives out fear, because fear has to do with punishment. The one who fears is not made perfect in love" (1 John 4:18).

Fear may come knocking at our doors; it may even try to say it has a familiar place in our lives. But we can serve fear its divorce papers because as long as we dwell in true love, it cannot tie itself to us any longer. Psalm 91 promises us many things when we consciously and pointedly choose to dwell in the shelter of the Most High:

> Surely he will save you from the fowler's snare and from the deadly pestilence. He will cover you with his feathers, and under his wings you will find refuge; his faithfulness will be your shield and rampart. You will not fear the terror of night,

nor the arrow that flies by day, nor the pestilence that stalks in the darkness, nor the plague that destroys at midday. A thousand may fall at your side, ten thousand at your right hand, but it will not come near you. (vv. 3–7)

What are we choosing to dwell in? Is it our fears or our circumstances? Do we dwell in negativity, unforgiveness, and offense? Do we dwell in our lack, pain, or bitterness? If so, these will become our shelter, refuge, and fortress if we continue to choose them over dwelling in the safe place of the Almighty. John 15 tells us to abide, remain in, and stay connected to Jesus, who is the vine. We are the branches of the vine, producing the fruit of life, as we stay connected to Him. God is our gardener pruning us and tending to our lives, as we remain connected to the Son.

Put Some Clothes On

Romans 13:13–14 says, "Let us behave decently, as in the daytime, not in carousing and drunkenness, not in sexual immorality and debauchery, not in dissension and jealousy. Rather, *clothe yourselves with the Lord Jesus Christ*, and do not think about how to gratify the desires of the flesh" (emphasis added). Okay, let's get super practical. In essence, these verses say we shouldn't do those things that obviously won't get us anything except a fortress of self-gratification. Rather, we must clothe ourselves with the Lord Jesus Christ.

In the Greek, clothing ourselves with Christ literally means to "get dressed in" Christ. We wouldn't just wake up in the morning and say, "You know what, I don't feel like wearing clothes to work today." I can pretty much guarantee that on our way to work, we would get arrested and thrown into jail. The truth is, when we don't "get dressed" in Christ, when we walk out of our homes "spiritually" naked, we get arrested by every power and principality that comes at us. Sometimes we wonder why we're so assaulted with dark thoughts, negative thinking, and fear. When we live with an acute awareness that we cannot be separated from the love of Christ (Rom. 8:38–39), we begin to come alive to the truth that we're wrapped in the love that casts out all fear. To clothe ourselves daily is to deny ourselves and submit again to His righteousness that covers us (Luke 9:23).

Combating Fear on a Practical Level

Here are three things we can start doing right now to combat fear practically.

Read the Word of God

Read the Bible—not so that you can follow a list of things you should do but so that you can know what is already yours. Reading God's words is all about the pursuit of His heart.

Read your Bible in partnership with the Holy Spirit. Allow Him to suggest your daily Scripture readings and to teach you about the heart of God behind each. I personally recommend reading Galatians in the Passion Translation, or read Matthew, Mark, Luke, or John and follow the life of Jesus in the Gospels. If you miss a day (or more), just pick your Bible back up without condemning yourself. Jesus isn't.

To know how God thinks and to learn the sound of His voice we have to read His words. They are more available to us now than they have ever been in history; any moment we choose, we can delve in. When we prioritize the Word of God, we will begin to understand His ways, thoughts, actions, and purposes for our lives. As we open up our heart to His life-giving words and nature, we will begin to put on Christ instead of our fears or worries.

Ingesting the "daily bread" from God will fuel our spirit, soul, and body so that when we are assaulted by the enemy's lies, we'll have the discernment to know, "Hey, wait a second, that's not how God speaks or thinks." We will be equipped to reject destructive ways of thinking.

> These words I speak to you are not incidental additions to your life, homeowner improvements to your standard of living. They are foundational words, words to build a life on. If you work these words into your life, you are like a smart carpenter who built his house on solid rock. Rain poured down, the river flooded, a tornado hit—but nothing moved that house. It was fixed to the rock. But if you just use my words in Bible studies and don't work them into your life, you are like a stupid carpenter who built his house on the sandy beach. When a storm rolled in and the waves came up, it collapsed like a house of cards. (Matt. 7:24–27 Message)

Our reading of the Word must also go beyond just that. Take time to meditate on it and massage it into the depths of our lives until we become like the word made flesh, as in John 1. God wants to build our lives up tall, but He can only build as high as the foundation is strong. Is your foundation secure, built on the words and ways of Jesus? Or is it built on sand? In this metaphor, what is sand? Sand is simply tiny bits of rock, but metaphorically speaking, sand is truth out of context—biblical passages abused to satisfy our distorted or selfish motives. Real truth is formed through the pursuit of God's heart, not just mental knowledge. Anything we build on sand will eventually collapse. Freedom comes when we implement the Word that brings life into our every moment. The Word is like food: when you eat it, it does what it's supposed to in our bodies and produces health, vitality, healing, wholeness, and life.

Pray, Meditate, and Connect to God

We often call our prayer time our "devotions" or "devotional." Devotion is a lifestyle, not a thirty-minute block of time during which we allow God to enter our lives each day. He is always present and available to talk and listen to. When Jesus breathed His last breath, the veil that separated us from God's presence was torn in two, granting each of us complete access to Him. That is a privilege we should never take for granted or sequester into a time slot. As you acknowledge His presence more and more in your life, you'll see true, deep, and meaningful transformation take place: "With all prayer and petition pray [with specific requests] at all times [on every occasion and in every season] in the Spirit, and with this in view, stay alert with all perseverance and petition [interceding in prayer] for all God's people" (Eph. 6:18 AMP).

Worship God

Psalm 103:1 says, "Praise the LORD, my soul; all my inmost being, praise his holy name." Worship isn't just for people with good voices, or four songs played to set up the message in a church service. It's something we put on as a lifestyle; it's our daily attitude of love for and surrender to God. When I am tormented or fearful, one of the first things I do is change the atmosphere around me. Often I turn on worship music and physically turn my face toward the heavens in acknowledgment of God's unending presence in my life. As I connect with who He is, while facing my fears, I can begin to hand them over, shifting and changing the atmosphere around me. Worship is putting worth on God, raising Him to the correct place of lordship in our lives. When we do this, we can more readily submit to the truth of Christ's gospel and allow Him to change us.

Charles Spurgeon wrote a beautiful exposition on the first verse of Psalm 103 in his book *The Treasury of David*. I pray that his words go deep into your spirit and cause you to rise up and give God all that you are, praising Him all the days of your life regardless of feelings or circumstances. He is worthy of our love, adoration, and praise! I truly believe that as worship becomes our chosen lifestyle, fear will begin to loose its authority to reside in the recesses of our spirit.

Bless the Lord O my soul. Soul music is the very soul of music. The Psalmist strikes the best keynote when he begins with stirring up his inmost self to magnify the Lord. He soliloquizes, holds self-communion and exhorts himself, as though he felt that dullness would all too soon steal over his faculties, as, indeed, it will over us all, unless we are diligently on the watch. Jehovah is worthy to be praised by us in that highest style of adoration which is intended by the term *bless*—"All thy works praise thee, O God, but thy saints shall bless thee." Our very life and essential self should be engrossed with this delightful service, and each one of us should arouse his own heart to the engagement. Let others forbear if they can: "Bless the Lord, O MY soul." Let others murmur, but do thou *bless*. Let others bless themselves and their idols, but do thou bless *the LORD*. Let others use only their tongues, but as for me I will cry, "Bless the Lord, O my *soul*." And all that is within me, bless his holy name. Many are our faculties, emotions, and capacities, but God has given them all to us, and they ought all to join in chorus to his praise. Half-hearted, ill-conceived, unintelligent praises are not such as we should render to our loving Lord. If the law of justice demanded all our heart and soul and mind for the Creator, much more may the law of gratitude put in a comprehensive claim for the homage of our whole being to the God of grace.[2]

Reading this causes me to want to shake off any apathy and stir up all that is within me to put my whole being into worshiping God, no matter how I feel, and to run into the arms of love.

I believe that when we continually apply these three practices in our lives, intentionally "putting on" Christ, things will begin to shift and change.

Some of you might be thinking this is all too simple and basic. Yes, maybe it is, but it works. We all have to choose to live out what life confronts us with on a daily basis We will face fears that will remain between God and us for eternity, but one thing I know is that as I have trusted in Him alone to be my refuge, fortress, and very present help in time of need, He has come through every time. He has protected and rescued me with His *deep love*. And because of that, I so deeply love Him.

"Because he loves me," says the LORD, "I will rescue him; I will protect him, for he acknowledges my name. He will call on me, and I will answer him; I will be with him in trouble, I will deliver him and honor him. With long life I will satisfy him and show him my salvation." (Ps. 91:14–16)

Remember, fear is a liar that only has the level of authority we give it. Starve it out by dwelling in and staying connected to God's perfect love. Recognizing and discerning fear is half the battle. Once you see it, you can take authority over it.

Truth: I am never separated from God's love; therefore fear cannot have authority in my life, unless I choose to partner with it.

▲ ◄ ◄ **Walking in Freedom** ► ► ▲

Grab your Bible and your journal (if you have one) and go to a place where you feel peaceful. For me, it's cozied up in my bed under the warm covers with a cup of coffee. Once you're settled, ask yourself these questions. Take your time, and be completely honest with yourself.

1. What fears are you knowingly or unknowingly partnering with and giving authority to at this stage in your life? Write them down.
2. Ask the Holy Spirit if He would like to take you to what opened the door to fear in the season you find yourself in. If yes, ask what He wants to show you. If no, let

it be and trust that God has the full process in hand. Come back to this question again at another time.

3. Now simply sit in God's presence. Close your eyes and picture the adoration that the Father, Son, and Holy Spirit have for you right in the middle of your fear. They are with you; can you picture them or feel them? What truth or promise are they handing you to actively combat fear and close the door to fear? What are you going to do with what they have given you?

4. Is there anyone you need to forgive for causing you to step into fear? Go to chapter 4, "Freedom from Unforgiveness," and use the forgiveness prayer tool.

5. Moving forward, what do you think you can do to make yourself aware of God's love rather than be fearful in a moment that feels overwhelming? What can you practically do to recognize that you are never disconnected or separated from His love (Rom. 8:38–39)?

6

Freedom from Anger

Let all bitterness and wrath and anger and clamor and slander be put away from you, along with all malice. Be kind to one another, tenderhearted, forgiving one another, as God in Christ forgave you.

Ephesians 4:31–32 ESV

Lie: I can control my world and those in it with anger. Anger protects me and keeps me safe.

It was the summer of 1985, and I was only seven years old when fits of anger started uncontrollably bubbling up from within me, quickly escalating into outright rage. I was physically and verbally violent with my siblings and resentful toward my mom and dad for everything they did. I acted as though we were on two separate teams, and my position was always defense. More often than not during that summer break, I would have a list of chores that would take me from sunup to sundown to complete—everything from pulling weeds to detail cleaning the bathroom—just so that I wouldn't lash out at someone. I needed to keep my hands busy and my mind preoccupied so that the hornet's nest inside me wouldn't get stirred up and attack everyone around me. Let's just say I had a lot of yelling and kicking matches with those weeds.

It was confusing and frustrating being so angry all the time at such a young age. I felt out of control, unable to restrain myself from lashing out at my family, and clueless as to the source of my emotions or the understanding to put an end to my outbursts. Now, having the advantage of hindsight after a journey to healing with Jesus, I can identify where unhealthy anger became my weapon of choice.

Healthy Anger Does Exist

Before we go any further, it's good to note that righteous anger does exist: "BE ANGRY, AND *yet* DO NOT SIN; do not let the sun go down on your anger, and do not give the devil an opportunity" (Eph. 4:26–27 NASB).

This passage implies that there is a form of anger that aligns with the heart of God, propelling us in the right direction with a passion to see change in our lives or the lives of those around us. It's an anger uncoupled from sin. Some anger is healthy, even necessary; other motivations of anger give the enemy an opportunity to destroy us, as well as those around us, and it's good for us to know the difference.

Healthy, righteous anger is appropriate when widows, orphans, and the helpless or marginalized are ignored or cast aside (Exod. 22:21–24; James 1:27). Righteous anger exists when those who should know better act as Pharisees, deceiving many while hardening their hearts toward the truth and way of the kingdom (Mark 3:5). Healthy anger is appropriate when people put roadblocks in the way of others stepping into the full redemption Jesus came to give (John 2:13–22). Anger is appropriate when the enemy steals, kills, destroys, or brings death in our lives or the lives of those around us (John 10:10). This is the type of anger that should move us to action. If we remain angry without appropriate action, it can become sin. Continue to check your heart and motives. It's important to remember that our battle is not against flesh and blood but against spiritual forces that seek to distort mindsets, bring deception, and separate from love (Eph. 6:12). It's good to know the difference between being mad at someone and being angry *for* someone.

Righteous anger exists to make a difference in the world, including our own personal world. We *should* have some healthy anger as we discover how ripped off we've been in certain areas of our lives. That's an anger that can fuel a fire strong enough to step into freedom. Just remember, healthy anger doesn't wound those we love nor make excuses for its actions. It's fuel to a fire that changes the world, motivating and enabling us to persevere through difficult tasks that would otherwise be wearing.

The Seed of Anger

So when did anger become my protector?

On two separate occasions when I was three and four years old, someone I should have been able to trust molested me. In those formative moments of my life, I unknowingly came into agreement with the lie that there was no one to protect me, so I would need to protect myself. At the young age of three, the weapon of anger was placed in my hands, and I began to practice wielding it with swift expertise. It was now my guardian, planted as a seed at an impressionable age, slowly and steadily growing into an insatiable monster.

When we offer our agreement willingly (even if unintentionally as a three- and four-year-old), the enemy need only plant a small seed—a thought or idea—that germinates and develops into a destructive mindset to ourselves and consequently affecting those in our world. When we are so young, not yet grown up in godly understanding, often hiding our issues from those who may offer guidance and healing because we don't know any better, even a small seed can make us prone to openly receive small lies as truth; then we allow them to develop and produce the fruit of death in our lives.

I didn't tell my mom until I was thirteen that I had been molested. She had taken me on a work road trip with her because I wasn't doing well at home or in school, and in the process of that drive the memories of what took place were revealed to me and consequently to her. For ten years my parents were unaware of the depths of the pain I had been carrying alone, and to be honest so was I. I had been trying to maneuver around my pain without any help from others except for the help of my close friend anger.

After the effects of sexual abuse left me confused and fearful, desperation rose in me for healthy male attention and protection. Unaware at the time of Father God's ability to cast away all of my fears in the pool of His love, I filled the void in countless ways—one of which was seeking and receiving male attention in any form I could get it—good, bad, and ugly.

When I gave my life to Jesus at nineteen, I stepped into a love that washed me so clean I hardly recognized myself. All my life I had known in my head that Jesus died for my sins, but I felt dirty and ashamed every time I sinned again, flogging myself with condemnation instead of stepping into love. At nineteen something shifted, and His love dropped from my head as a concept and enveloped my heart; a new seed began to germinate.

The good news for every single one of us is this: because of God's kindness, goodness, and love for us, He sent His son Jesus to destroy death and bring life to any area in which we have adopted a destructive mindset or way of living. He is the way, the truth, and the life that we are looking for. He is the way into the arms of God. He is the *way* of living that brings healing and restoration, He is the *truth* that changes who we are, and He is the very essence of *life* that conquers any death we may face (John 14:6).

Fast-Forward: Marriage

In the years leading up to marriage, my relationship with Jesus was blissful and beautiful. Many nights I would light candles, turn on worship music, and bask in His company for hours on end. I had only been saved four years before I met my husband; we were married on July 27, 2002. After marrying Paul, I unconsciously put him in the place of the healer, expecting him to be the one to redeem all of the mistakes that the men in my past made. My relational brokenness with men was rising to the surface, and I wanted my husband to fix it. That didn't work out so well.

Paul was born and raised in Sydney, Australia, while I was born and raised in Spokane, Washington. On our wedding day, two worlds collided under the covenant of marriage with two persons of *completely* different upbringing. Granted, we were both from English-speaking households, but our cultures and environments growing up were very different. Paul had come from a family that really never argued. He can't remember a time when his parents had a disagreement in front of him, and if anyone did get angry, for the most part, it would get stopped in its formative stages and the "peace" would be kept. The Andrew household (before I came into the picture) was like Switzerland: neutral ground where anger was kept in a safe-deposit box. In contrast, my parents nearly got divorced and fought it out in front of us, and as a result my siblings and I never avoided processing every emotion in public. We let it all hang out, leaving everything on the table during heated exchanges. Both households were extreme, and neither particularly healthy, which left a huge learning curve in our fledgling marriage when it came to conflict resolution.

Marriage awakened the sleeping monster within me in more ways than one, and my then-confused husband wondered if he was married to the same girl he had met a year earlier and fallen in love with. Being in the same house all the time and becoming one flesh with someone who thinks, sleeps, washes the dishes, and squeezes the toothpaste tube differently than you has an uncanny way of pushing all your buttons and bringing all sorts of issues to the surface—not to mention my unspoken expectation of Paul fixing my problems. Dating was, for the most part, romantic and bliss-ful. With that said, half of it was long distance, so we really only got to know each other through phone calls and emails. We didn't have enough time to deeply discover each other, in all our many imperfections, before we got engaged (which happened to be on top of the Eiffel Tower at sunset). Our engagement was a quick six months, and before I knew it, we were married!

Becoming One

What I have learned is that in marriage we become one with someone, we belong to each other body, soul, and spirit. A divine intertwining takes place, as we become "one flesh"; we are a representation of the image of God—the Trinity. Remember, God created Adam *and* Eve, as well as you and me, in His image: "So God created mankind in his own image, in the image of God he created them; male and female he created them" (Gen. 1:27).

So when two of God's beloved creations made in His image become *one flesh*, you better believe that issues will come to the surface, giving ample opportunity to either deal with them head on or let them bring division. Because the Godhead does not consist of issues, when we come together in marriage, we have opportunity after opportunity to be refined to *reflect* His likeness. Our intimacy and proximity to one another force underlying issues to the surface and cause marriage to be a refining fire that will either bring out the gold or burn us up. Both parties must be committed to going through the refining fire—no matter what, commit-ted to becoming one: "'For this reason a man will leave his father and mother and be united to his wife, and the two will become one flesh.' So they are no longer two, but one flesh. Therefore what God has joined together, let no one separate" (Mark 10:7–9).

Satan will try to separate us from God and from those we love. Marriage is one of the most powerful weapons forged against the kingdom of darkness. We need to understand as we walk into it that it will refine us and bring us closer to God and one another if we let it. Both Satan and God want to make us like them. To conform to the image of Satan is to become selfish and sin-conscious. To conform to the image of God is to become love and Jesus-conscious.

I remember one particular time when I picked a fight with Paul on purpose. This was becoming a regular occurrence, but I remember this instance because of what he said to me. He looked straight at me and said with a stern, unrelenting expression, "Andi—I will never fight with you." To which I laughed in his face, tilted my head, and gave him the biggest Cheshire cat smile. He had kicked the hornet's nest, and it was on. I would do everything in my power to get him to fight with me—everything!

And Then Came Children

Having kids only served to exacerbate the violent stirring within. I was out of control. Four little sticks were added to the poking and prodding, releasing the monster on a more consistent basis. I've heard it said, "Marriage shows you how selfish you are, and children show you how angry you are." Unfortunately for my family, this statement was proved true.

Children are innocent little beings that need you twenty-four hours a day, seven days a week. When you're tired, they need you. When you want time for yourself, they need you. When you want to go to the bathroom alone, they need you. If you're someone who hasn't dealt with your anger problems, children will push your every button until you either get it together or lapse into someone you never thought you'd become.

I have a poignant memory of a particular morning in our household when Zeke was only three years old, Jesse was one, and our daughter, Finley, had just been born. With three kids under the age of three, my hormones were in a tailspin. I felt as though I needed my coffee given to me intravenously and a therapist on speed dial—or better yet, in residence at the Andrew household. Needless to say, Paul and I were going through a rough season.

The morning began normally. I was down in the kitchen making breakfast for the kids, and Paul was making our much-needed coffee. I had spent the whole evening prior meticulously cleaning up the house, to the point of obsession. Cleanliness and control made me feel safe and sane. Every toy had its own place in the playroom, every chair around the dining table was perfectly spaced, every pillow on the couch was fluffed and angled with care, and not a mark or crumb was left on our floor. Then I heard *the sound*. It was the sound that I permitted to drive me into a fit of rage. Zeke, my three-year-old toddler, had taken the box of Legos and dumped them on my just-vacuumed carpet in *my* immaculately organized toy room.

In one moment, I transformed from a calm mother making breakfast for her kids to a venomous snake lashing out at my son for playing with his toys . . . for playing with his toys! Fear pierced his heart as I ripped him to shreds with my words. The look of fear in his eyes should have brought me to my knees in repentance, but it didn't. I persisted, hurling words that wounded my baby boy. For a split second, out of the corner of my eye, I caught my husband's look of total disbelief, which was enough to shock the monster back into its cage, releasing a wave of shame. It felt like something was taking over my body, and this unhealthy anger was quickly becoming a normal part of my life.

I confessed to love my son, yet I was mad at him for behaving like any child would. Was I going crazy? It sure felt like it. Paul asked me to go up to our room, knowing I needed to take my anger out before God, not on those I loved the most.

I remember the walk of shame up to my room. I turned away from my family and started sobbing, overrun with grief over this way too familiar "thing" that had control over my life. While it had always been there to a degree, this was different. It was starting to scare me. The trauma of a difficult season had brought a new level of anger out of its cage. With a husband and children in the picture, I decided I couldn't allow it to have its way with me anymore. They didn't deserve this and neither did I. I realized, however, that I didn't know how to stop being angry because it had been my weapon of defense for so long. In all its destruction, it was familiar and comfortable. I didn't know how to let God fight for me, protect me, or heal me, and I began to question my very worth. I was allowing the man who abused me when I was an innocent toddler to speak more loudly about my value than Jesus.

I went up into my room and let my pillows have it, punching them while yelling expletives loud enough for the neighborhood to hear. When I had finished my tirade, I apologized to God for not trusting Him with my heart, for hurting my son, and for scaring my family. I apologized for being someone I knew He didn't create me to be, and I told Him I wanted to change but didn't know how.

After sitting in the Father's love and ranting in utter honesty, I came back down the stairs as calm and collected as I possibly could with puffy red eyes, ringing my hands until they felt raw, hoping that my family would accept me after my impressive display. What I saw broke my heart into a thousand pieces. Zeke was standing there, with a big nervous smile on his face, saying to me, "See, Mummy, see . . . I cleaned it all up. I'm so sorry, Mummy. I cleaned it up."

I broke. Shaking, I fell to my knees and wrapped him in my arms, hiding my face from him while tears uncontrollably spilled down my face.

"No, Mummy is sorry. It's okay for you to play with your toys; that's what they're here for. Mummy is sorry for getting so mad at you. Will you forgive me?"

And in his cute little voice with an Australian twang he said, "Yes, Mummy." We just sat there and hugged as I let out silent sobs of repentance, still unsure of the way out of this insatiable anger that was damaging those I loved the most. I knew in that moment, if I didn't start to work my issues out, I was going to bring up children that needed to tiptoe around me and please me so that the "beast" wouldn't come out to play.

I was a grown woman, with a free will and complete access to God's healing love, yet totally out of control, working so hard to receive the love that was already mine! I knew there was freedom for me, but it seemed so far off and unattainable. I was grasping but with no real hold on how. Deep down, I knew it wasn't God's character to dangle a carrot in my face and never let me partake of it, because He is kind and good. I now realize I had a broken view of God at the time. I believed the lie that He hadn't protected me all those years ago so I needed to protect myself with my anger, even if it wasn't working. It was all I knew to do.

Finding Truth

Anger may keep us *feeling* safe, but it's a counterfeit. We'll feel safe only temporarily because anger slowly erodes trust and destroys connection. Real safety is being rescued from death by a selfless king, One who forgave us and showed us the way to remain tenderhearted and forgiving and in turn empowered us with the ability to put off anger, wrath, bitterness, and the like! Remember this? "Let all bitterness and wrath and anger and clamor and slander be put away from you, along with all malice. Be kind to one another, tenderhearted, forgiving one another, as God in Christ forgave you" (Eph. 4:31–32 ESV).

After the Lego tirade, I felt the Holy Spirit whisper to me, "When you're angry, you rob value from those who receive the brunt of your rage. When you act like that, you are telling them that they're not worth love and that they don't matter. Your selfish protective mechanisms only matter in that moment." Not only is anger damaging, it's selfish and self-preserving.

I learned another valuable lesson that day: *anger erodes trust and doesn't bring honor.* Honor and value go hand in hand. The Greek word for honor is *timé* meaning "a valuing, a price, honor"[1] or a "perceived value or worth."[2] In essence, to bring honor to someone or something is "a valuing"; to place value on something or someone brings honor. How much do I honor and value those in my world? How much do I value my heart and life? Is it enough to see lasting change?

Over the years, I've learned and come into agreement with the truth that I am extremely valuable. I am worth the sacrifice that came to rescue me. I am worth love. I need to constantly align myself with this truth; I am valued and celebrated enough to receive the love that came to live within my heart and trade in my anger. And what about those around me? They are so unbelievably valuable and loved! They are worth giving my love to. But to become love I need to receive it first (Mark 12:30–31)!

Do you carry the weight of anger? Is it your protector? Friend, Jesus died to carry the weight of your anger upon Himself and to bind up your broken heart. He is willing to do these for you daily whenever and wherever anger takes hold. We've got to ask ourselves, why does anger have authority in our lives? Where was the door opened to let anger in? Was it a specific moment or memory? Because God created time, He is not confined to it. He can span time and space to heal us of any moment, memory, trauma, or pain that caused anger to be our self-defense mechanism. Don't box God in. He is not a man—He is God—the very being of love, the love that can set us free from anger.

Dealing with the Root

When did I take the reins of my life and stop trusting God? The answer lies with that three-year-old girl.

About a year after moving to New York City, through some time in prayer, I pinpointed the moment when my trust in God was broken (by Satan). It was the moment I took the reins of control into my own hands because I was afraid I wouldn't be protected. In turn, I forged the weapon of anger to keep me safe, because I believed the lie that God didn't. Countless incidents thereafter, in which I lacked control over my circumstances or the way people treated or perceived me, only confirmed my distrust in God and a growing investment in my self-preserving choices. The weapon of damaging anger became more difficult to contain as I grew older.

In a prayer time seeking to deal with the underlying root of my pain, anger, and control, I fell to the floor and cried out to God in desperation, "Where were you when I needed you? How could you abandon me?"

And as peaceful and calm as a tender Father whose heart was broken at seeing firsthand His daughter's abuse and pain, He whispered, *I was there. My heart was broken as I witnessed free will, my gift to all mankind, being used to cause you suffering. Free will was made to bring love, but some choose to live for themselves, using it for evil. On that day, Satan came to destroy your trust in Me. Your purpose in this life is of great value, so your enemy will use any means possible to take you out. He has come only to rob, kill, and destroy. But do not fear, I have overcome with great love.*

I broke down in sobs. The root of this prickly, ugly vine that had entangled my heart and affected every area of my life was gently loosened and pulled out of me in an instant of divine revelation through God's persistent, ever-present love. That love and revelation were only found by acknowledging the presence (of which there is no substitute) of the One who gave of Himself to rescue me from the destroyer. We were always meant for Him . . . for His love. He rescued me! He loves me! He's my protector, not anger! I came into agreement with this truth and still do so every day.

As I lay there on the floor, my limbs began to feel light, tingling in their newfound freedom, no longer weighed down by rage. I was relieved of an inner churning that had been boring a hole in my heart, causing it to beat callously toward God. Staring at the ceiling in awe, still reverberating from fresh revelation, I asked for God to make me aware of His always-present love in me and fill the void that was left when the familiar roots of fear, anger, and control were ripped out. He responded willingly, flooding my inmost being with His manifest love.

While this story describes my personal moment of revelation, be encouraged that we are all ripe for powerful encounters and moments at any time with our tender, loving God who became a catalyst for freedom. After we receive a revelation that brings freedom, we then have stewardship responsibility to live in it. It's like being given an inheritance— we can squander it or we can cultivate it. How do we remain in our freedom? We do so by living present and aware of our unending connection to Him. Remember, we cannot be separated from His love (Rom. 8:38–39). I can honestly say that anger is an unfamiliar weapon for me now. When it comes out, I quickly look within to see when I stopped trusting, what I'm afraid of, or what has pushed my buttons and why I'm protecting myself. I acknowledge His unending love and allow it to heal my heart once again. His love truly casts out all fear.

The Fruit of the Spirit

When it comes to diffusing the bomb that is anger, it's an inside job. Anger is the fruit of pain. Once the pain is acknowledged and healed with love through connection to the healer and by walking in forgiveness, repentance, and revelation, or by the cutting off and replacement of lies through God's truths, it's time to cultivate our new reality with an awareness of what we've already been given—the fruit of the Spirit. In a garden, if a plant is left untended, it will die. So it is with our hearts; they require consistent attention, nurturing, tending, and pruning.

To continue the metaphor, our heart can be likened to soil (Matt. 13:19), and our humility and openness allow the Holy Spirit's constant presence and leading to be like the nutrients and water that penetrate the soil. Imagine the Holy Spirit as a constant source of nourishment and fresh water, ready to till and work the soil of our hearts and care for what has been deposited from heaven within us: "But the fruit of the Spirit is love, joy, peace, patience, kindness, goodness, faithfulness, gentleness, self-control; against such things there is no law. And those who belong to Christ Jesus have crucified the flesh with its passions and desires" (Gal. 5:22–24 ESV). Cultivating the fruit of the Spirit is just that. It's an intentional choice to be led by the Holy Spirit to nurture what God has already given us in Jesus—love, joy, peace, patience, kindness, goodness, faithfulness, gentleness, and self-control. We are new creations when we are born again, and our inheritance, or our gift at rebirth, is the fruit of the Spirit.

When we see these things growing in our lives, it's because we've been intentional with what has been deposited within us. The fruit of the Spirit *is* our nature in Christ! It is evidence that the Spirit of God is transforming our lives and causing us to flourish in our divine partnership.

In our house, we have a marble jar for each of our kids. Any time we catch them operating in the fruit of the Spirit, we give them a marble. When their marble jar is full, they receive a reward and some quality time with Mom and Dad. This causes them to live with an awareness of the nature they already have in Jesus. When we choose engagement and connection to love instead of anger, joy instead of anger, peace instead of anger, patience instead of anger, kindness instead of anger, goodness instead of anger, faithfulness instead of anger, gentleness instead of anger, and self-control instead of anger, we can't help but be transformed and walk in the righteous life that God desires for us. We will find ourselves aligned with the righteousness that has been given to us through Jesus's life, death, and resurrection and walking in the territory of freedom that God has always intended for us to live in through His Son. I've heard righteousness defined as "right standing before God"; Jesus paid the price so that we could stand before God in right relationship with Him.

We each have a free will and the ability to choose what we will feed, cultivate, and step into. We can choose death or we can choose life. As we align ourselves with the healer, bringing Him our pain while continuously choosing to put on Christ and operate in the fruit of the Spirit, we'll find anger becoming more and more a foreign weapon of choice as love takes over.

....

Truth: Anger is a counterfeit bodyguard. God, who is
   love, rescues me, protects me, and heals my heart in

and through every season. His love is always present in my life.

....

Walking in Freedom

1. Find a safe place to connect with the Father, Son, and Holy Spirit. When you're quiet, ask yourself: Was there an experience or experiences that caused me to adapt a warped belief system? Have I allowed anger to dwell in and protect my heart? Write down what you hear, feel, and think.

2. Take authority over the lie and break it off in your life. It was your choice (whether conscious or unconscious) to agree with it, and it is your choice to part ways with it, through the grace and presence of God. Remember, your authority is in Jesus's name, not yours. Feel free to use the following as a guideline, but pray sincerely out of your own heart: "*Anger, I take authority over you, in the name of Jesus Christ, and the lie that I have believed that you would protect me better than Jesus would. Right now, I send you to the foot of the cross where Jesus will deal with you as He sees fit. In Jesus's name, amen!*" You may need to repent for letting your anger protect you instead of God. You can use the forgiveness prayer found in chapter 4. Repentance and forgiveness are the everyday tools needed to live free on a daily basis.

3. Ask what truth God would like to give you in place of the lie you have believed. Write down what you hear.

4. In prayer, hold out your hands as a prophetic gesture of receiving that truth that has been given to you. Put a reminder of that truth in a place where you can see it so that you can be reminded to walk in it daily.

5. Read and write out Galatians 5:22–24 in your favorite translation of the Bible. In partnership with the Holy Spirit, meditate on what it looks like to cultivate this fruit in your personal life. Decide now to practice operating in and intentionally cultivating the fruit of the Spirit.

7

Freedom from Shame

The Spirit of the Lord God is upon me, . . . to proclaim the favorable year of the Lord. . . . Instead of your [former] shame *you will have* a double portion; and *instead* of humiliation your people will shout for joy over their portion. Therefore in their land they will possess double [what they had forfeited]; everlasting joy will be theirs."

Isaiah 61:1, 2, 7 AMP

Lie: I will live with this shame for the rest of my life. Keeping the ugly things hidden protects me and keeps me safe from public opinion and rejection.

Shame is an ugly place of disgrace and dishonor causing us to live without the knowledge of our value and worth. It comes in various forms. The shame that lingers from your past is like the decaying remnants of death and is accompanied by a stench of fear. It reminds you of who you used to be and rots away any hope that you'll ever get to live fully in your purpose. Maybe the shame comes from lies and rumors that have been spoken about you and believed by the multitude. The way others look at you when you walk into a room makes you suspicious that everyone "knows" and is talking about you, even when they are not. Shame is mean like that. It could be sexual shame as you once again look at pornography "just one last time." And the blanket of shame covers you as you settle under the weight of it again. It could be shame from the abortion or abortions you've had, and you are riddled with fear to tell anyone because you believe you deserve hell for what you've done. You don't. There is a love that desires to connect with you in the darkest crevices of your life. It's a love that can heal you and set you free.

Shame gradually destroys your connection to God and in turn your connection to others. Shame is one of the biggest hindrances to true and lasting intimacy—intimacy between you and God and intimacy with others. We were created to be in connection and in loving community. It has never been good for us to be alone.

Some of you may be thinking, *Well that's fine because I don't really want to be close to anyone anyway. I don't really need people because they've always let me down, and I've been fine on my own.* Have you? Deep down, often the real reason you think this way is this: if you do let people close, they may see the real you and not like what they see—because you don't like what you see.

Getting Stuck in the Mud of Shame

An unfortunate familiarity with shame came into my life at the same time anger and fear did. The enemy's assignments against my parents brought a tangible instability for me as a child causing insecurity to rise and turning me into a vacuum for affection from my father. In that season, however, he was preoccupied with his own pain, desperately needing Healer God as much as I did. The damages left behind from sexual abuse were permitted to remain, leaving a crack in the door of my life for shame to seep in.

Starving for affection, I experimented sexually because it provided a hit of counterfeit love and intimacy. Yet every time, I felt absolute shame for my actions and kept them hidden. Somehow, I knew it was wrong. At fifteen, I gave the gift of my virginity away, and then repeatedly had sex until I gave my life to Jesus at nineteen. The sex made me *feel* loved, yet a vortex remained, sucking up any hope of lifelong commitment or promise of unending covenant love. Sex had become a counterfeit, void of intimacy and commitment, that bred a deep fear of abandonment and heavy shame.

Just as sexual experimentation gave way to sex, sex gave way to pornography, and pornography opened up another door for more shame to wrap around me. I began dabbling in drugs, though nothing heavy, which provided another hit of counterfeit elation but, you guessed it, piled more shame on top of me. To make matters worse, I endured the trauma of walking through my pain publically, while opinions and gossip ran wild. Such talk is the mud that the devil washes his hands in and smears all over us, reminding us with a vindictive, repetitive whisper that we're damaged, rejected, and unworthy, just like everyone is saying.

Shame taught me to isolate myself from others, even my husband. It wasn't conscious at first, but because I believed so many lies, I assumed that I would never have freedom in my life. I began to believe I was a reject who needed to spare the world of my presence. As each day, week, month, and year passed that I didn't deal with the root of my shame, the enemy continued to accuse and pile it on—for as long as I would let him derail my destiny.

Can I Just Run Away from All This?

It wasn't long after we planted Liberty Church in New York that I felt a need to run away from the city, which in hindsight I now connect to the heavy cloak of shame that was spiritually draped around my shoulders. I had given it permission to remain there by leaning into every lie whispered in my ear, receiving it like some sort of penance I felt I deserved. I remember that feeling of wanting to run and never return. The compounded undealt-with issues from my past began taking their toll on me, as well as those around me. I no longer desired sex or to be touched by my husband, and I didn't want any close friends. I was becoming a recluse and keeping everyone at arm's length; intimacy was my enemy. I believed the lie that my isolation was beneficially keeping others "safe" from me.

The truth is, Satan is the destroyer of intimacy and love, and his destructive words are always accompanied by shame. Let's see him for who he is: jealous of our connection to God through Jesus and with His beloved creation made in His image.

In that particular season, most people who heard me preach or had a conversation with me thought I was the most fun-loving person in the room. God has created me to bring joy to those in my life! But on the inside, I'd long ago adopted false mindsets about how disgusting and damaged I was. I was deathly afraid that if people really got to know me, they would see my broken mess. As a lead pastor, that didn't seem like an option. I didn't even want to go to church most Sundays because people were there—the church we were pastoring! I simply felt overwhelmed.

I remember saying to Paul, "Look, I know God called us here. I really do love these people, but I am riddled with shame and fear, which are hamstringing my ability to love anybody let alone myself into healthy community and wholeness. I need to get out of here. Don't worry, I'll come back . . . but I can't live like this. Something has to change in me."

Paul "Steady as He Goes" Andrew lovingly replied, "Anything, babe. What would help you?"

I already knew what I wanted to do. I said, "Well, I know that in a few weeks, my sister's church in Seattle is having a women's conference. No one knows me there except my sister and her pastor, Wendy. It would be a safe place where I can let go and hear from God."

Immediately after our conversation, we booked the tickets and I prepared my heart to let God into the places I had locked up. I didn't know exactly what was about to happen, but I didn't really care. I was desperate, and I knew that the way I was living was neither God's plan nor purpose for my life.

When my sister picked me up in Seattle, I noticed immediately that she carried a peace with her that began to crack the walls I had built around my heart. We hugged each other lovingly and drove to the hotel in silence. We settled in, got dressed, and went to the conference.

I don't remember how many sessions in we were, but I remember Wendy Treat was speaking on forgiveness. I had dismissed the message in my mind, assuming this wasn't "the one" I came to hear. After all, I was dealing with shame and crippling fear. Clearly I needed a message on that topic. How wrong I was!

As Wendy finished up her message and transitioned into some time to pray for people, she said, "If you're dealing with unforgiveness come up to the front and our prayer team is here to pray with you." I remained in my chair, praying for all those people with forgiveness issues because, of course, I wasn't one of them. That's when I felt "the nudge," which I tried to ignore, but my pulse began to rise, adrenaline surging through my veins and my heart nearly leaping out of my throat. God whispered, "Go up."

I replied under my breath, "No God! I'm not dealing with unforgiveness! I need to be set free from shame and fear! I will wait for the appropriate altar call, or I'm not going. I don't need people judging me thinking I'm an unforgiving woman!"

"Go up."

"No."

"Go up."

"Fine. But this isn't my issue."

I grabbed my sister's hand and asked if she would come with me. She smiled and put her hand on my back, walking next to me down the aisle. The moment we got to the front, she laid both hands on my back, began to pray for me, and I hit the floor . . . hard. Embarrassingly hard. My body felt like it had caught on fire and was tingling like crazy everywhere. I abandoned all pride and began wailing at the top of my lungs, flat on my face before God and every woman at that conference. Apparently to be set free from shame, I really needed to let go of what everyone thought of me.

As I lay there on my face with my sister's arms around me, I felt the presence of two large hands sweeping down and lifting a heavy, dirty cloak off of my shoulders. I envisioned myself naked on the floor as the cloak of shame was lifted off of me by my rescuer's mighty hands. Immediately after, I saw two big wings come and cover me, and a voice from heaven said, "She who dwells in the shelter of the Most High will find rest in the shadow of My wings. I will cover you. Shame has no hold on you."

Remember, there is no substitute for the presence of God to which we have access at all times. Forgiveness lets us out of prison and on a journey to freedom and restorations. Forgiveness opens the door to walk into healing. Jesus's love and forgiveness give us access to our healing. What He has the ability to do in us and for us as we dwell there is powerful; we only need acknowledge what we already have.

One of my favorite Scriptures came to mind that day:

He who dwells in the secret place of the Most High shall remain stable *and* fixed under the shadow of the Almighty [whose power no foe can withstand]. I will say of the Lord, He is my Refuge and my Fortress, my God; on Him I lean *and* rely, *and* in Him I [confidently] trust! For [then] He will deliver you from the snare of the fowler and from the deadly pestilence. [Then] He will cover you with His pinions, and under His wings shall you trust *and* find refuge; His truth *and* His faithfulness are a shield and a buckler. (Ps. 91:1–4 AMP-CE)

I had been suddenly and powerfully delivered from shame in that moment, swept up in a vision in which I was covered under Almighty God's wings, finding refuge in the only one in whom I can put all my trust. I felt Him say to me, "You can trust Me; I will cover you and deliver you from your shame. I will not embarrass you, nor will I harm you."

Lying there, I became innately aware of the song being sung over the women, a song about how much God loves us—over and over again. His love was ringing in my ears, pulsating through my veins, covering me in my nakedness, and I felt no shame for the first time in years. In a moment in which I could have felt embarrassed for lying on the floor looking like an absolute fool, I experienced one of the safest moments of my lifetime, wrapped in my Father's arms, protected from every accusation and plan of and attack from the enemy. I wanted to stay. The good news is, I can because He never leaves me: "Do not fear, for you will not be put to shame, and do not feel humiliated or ashamed, for you will not be disgraced. For you will forget the shame of your youth" (Isa. 54:4 AMP).

I love that in the midst of a season when I tried to isolate myself from others, I found myself safe in the arms of my sister's love. She grew up with me, knew all my ugly, dirty secrets, and still loved me by choice. She was a safe place and still is to this day. I didn't even need to talk to her—her presence alone helped bring me freedom. Her unconditional love helped break down barriers so God could do what only He can do—bind up my broken heart and remove all my shame.

The Woman with the Issue of Blood

The woman with the issue of blood dealt with shame in immeasurable ways. She was bleeding and therefore, in Hebrew culture, "unclean" for twelve years. Within those twelve years she would have been secluded and cut off from society, ridiculed and alone, void of connection. According to Jewish law (Lev. 12:1–8; 15:19–30), when a woman was bleeding she was unclean and impure, whether that be her monthly period, the month of bleeding that occurs after birth, or hemorrhaging like the woman with the issue of blood. She couldn't have sex with her husband (if she had one) and had to be isolated from society and regular fellowship. She could not worship God in the temple, and when walking around in public she would have to declare that she was unclean. This would have been extremely embarrassing, isolating, and humiliating. When she heard that Jesus was passing through town, her desperation for healing superseded her shame. She risked public ridicule and the possibility of making others unclean to see him:

> A woman was there who had been subject to bleeding for twelve years. She had suffered a great deal under the care of many doctors and had spent all she had, yet instead of getting better she grew worse. When she heard about Jesus, she came up behind him in the crowd and touched his cloak, because she thought, "If I just touch his clothes, I will be healed." Immediately her bleeding stopped and she felt in her body that she was freed from her suffering.

At once Jesus realized that power had gone out from him. He turned around in the crowd and asked, "Who touched my clothes?"

"You see the people crowding against you," his disciples answered, "and yet you can ask, 'Who touched me?'"

But Jesus kept looking around to see who had done it. Then the woman, knowing what had happened to her, came and fell at his feet and, trembling with fear, told him the whole truth. He said to her, "Daughter, your faith has healed you. Go in peace and be freed from your suffering." (Mark 5:25–34)

To go from captivity to freedom, we must humble ourselves like the woman with the issue of blood and say, "I don't care what the cost is and I no longer care what people think; I will do whatever it takes to get free from this bondage." We must have the tenacity to push through and touch Jesus even when others tell us to give up.

Reach Out for Jesus

Maybe like the woman with the issue of blood, who was separated from society and isolated from God's presence, you feel isolated and alone in your shame. The loss of blood and the repercussions of her condition would have left her exhausted, weak, anemic, and spiritually dry. The long sickness could have made her feel overwhelmed and alone on her journey, and the same could be true for you in what you're facing.

She had spent all her money trying to find healing. The passage also says she "suffered" at the hands of many doctors and only grew worse. So not only was she broke, but she also got sicker as each year passed. In the area where you need to be freed from shame, are you going from person to person "spending" all that you have but receiving only Band-Aid solutions that aren't fixing the problem? Maybe you've been let down so many times by people that you find it hard to push through the throng of voices and trust God, The only thing that can bring you true healing is to reach out and receive from Jesus.

The touching of the hem of Jesus's garment is significant. The part of the fabric the woman touched is known as the tallit, or prayer shawl. Fringes or tassels were to be sewn on the four corners of all clothing of Jewish men in accordance with God's instruction:

> The LORD said to Moses, "Speak to the Israelites and say to them: 'Throughout the generations to come you are to make tassels on the corners of your garments, with a blue cord on each tassel. You will have these tassels to look at and so you will remember all the commands of the LORD, that you may obey them and not prostitute yourselves by chasing after the lusts of your own hearts and eyes. Then you will remember to obey all my commands and will be consecrated to your God. I am the LORD your God, who brought you out of Egypt to be your God. I am the LORD your God.'" (Num. 15:37–41)

The tassels were to remind the Jewish people of God's commandments. They were tied into 613 knots to remind them of the 613 laws of Moses: 365 "thou shalt not" laws and 248 "thou shalt" laws. The tassels were in full view for everyone to see as a constant reminder to walk in God's ways, to stay on His path of righteousness.

When Jewish men were deep in prayer, they would wear this prayer shawl over their heads to be covered in the presence of God. The shawls were white and blue. The white represents heaven—the dwelling place of the Lord—and the blue represents the Holy Spirit.

The tallit also represents authority. King David was known as a man after God's own heart (Acts 13:22), but before he became king, the reigning King Saul wanted to murder him. David had an opportunity for revenge in a cave. David's cohorts, also known as his "Mighty Men," encouraged him to kill King Saul (1 Sam. 24:1–7). Instead, he snuck up behind Saul and cut the hem of his garment, yet was "conscience stricken" for doing so because it was an act that represented him cutting off the authority of his king. When Ruth laid down at Boaz's feet, she placed herself under his tallit or his authority to submit herself to him (Ruth 3:1–9).

When this woman who had lived a life of shame and reproach for twelve years reached out to touch Jesus, she didn't grab just what happened to be at arm's length. She was going to make this count if she was going to go out into the crowd and risk making others unclean by physically touching them as she pushed through to her healer. She also risked making a rabbi (Jesus) unclean. As I read this account, I wonder if she knew the significance of touching His tallit. I'd like to think she did, because when she reached out to touch the hem of His garment, she reached out for all it represented—all the promises and commandments from the Word of God, God's covering and His presence, and all the authority of heaven and earth that Jesus was given as God's Son. The tallit or the hem of His garment represents God's commandments, the presence of God, and God's authority!

When you reach out to God for your healing and deliverance, realize that you are touching all the promises of the Word of God—every commandment He has given. And that Word became flesh and made His dwelling among us—you are touching Him! Realize that you're touching the covering of His presence and all of the authority that is in heaven and earth through the power of Jesus Christ.

When she touched Jesus, *immediately* He felt power go out of Him. When you reach out and touch Him, it doesn't just affect your life in miraculous ways; He feels your touch too. He turns his face to you, acknowledges and adores you in your public shame, heals you, and commends your faith in Him. He says to you, "Daughter, your faith has made you well" (Mark 5:34), or in other words, "Your *trust* in me has made you well."

The heart of Father God is that you would understand that through your faith (the substance of things hoped for, the evidence of things not yet seen [Heb. 11:1]) in Jesus, you are healed *and* brought into the family—you are God's daughter! As a daughter, you are an heir to all Jesus has—healing, love, freedom, eternal life, redemption, restoration of all that was lost, and so much more.

Jesus is the Prince of Peace, and your faith, trust, and hope in Him heals you and connects you to all that He is and has.

Back to the Garden

Isolation that leads to shame is the serpent's age-old trick; he's been doing it since the Garden of Eden. If we're not savvy enough to be aware of his tricks, he will try the same thing with us over and over. If he can get us to believe the lie that we are separated from God's love and out of the presence of our Father, he can get us to see that we are naked and look foolish. But God created us to be completely free in front of Him, warts and all. The devil wants to prove that we're like him, but that's where he is wrong. We were created in the image of God.

We all live out of our belief systems and give or withhold out of our identities. Often, we form our identities out of many sources: who we think we are, who others say we are, and who we think God says we are. In truth, the solidity of our identities is directly correlated with our connection to God and our understanding of His character. Intimacy and trust in our God comes as He breaks unhealthy belief systems and cleanses the dirty, shameful, and broken places of our lives—this is how we are perfected in His love.

We can view the world and the Word of God through our experiences and our reaction to them, and at times our insecurities, fears, and pain dirty the lenses of our viewpoints and hold us back from uninhibited connection to God, the source of all life and reality. Jesus came to restore all that was lost in the Garden of Eden. He came so that I could walk in my redemptive potential, the way God has always seen me as He knit me together in my mother's womb. Yet because of our past, many of us are viewing God through an unhealthy lens that is negatively affecting our identities and causing us to live in shame.

From the very beginning, God gave us free will. God formed man from the dirt and breathed His image, "the breath of life," into us (Gen. 1:26–27, 2:7) for a purpose: to reproduce His image and cover the earth in His glory

(Gen. 1:28). In the Garden of Eden, there were two trees: one that gave eternal and everlasting life and one that brought death (the knowledge of good and evil). One of them we were free to eat from—the tree of life; the other was forbidden because it brought eternal death, destruction, and separation from God (Gen. 2:8–9, 15–17). When Adam and Eve were deceived into eating from the tree of the knowledge of good and evil, which God promised would surely kill them (Gen. 2:17), the very first result described was that "they realized they were naked" (Gen. 3:7). So the killing God had spoken of was the death of His image in them—His Spirit—and the fruit of spiritual death was self-consciousness. For just one chapter earlier, the Bible notes, "Adam and his wife were both naked, and they felt no shame." (Gen. 2:25). From that point on, mankind was born into the sin of Adam, choosing to live according to our own righteousness and forced to toil for protection and provision—no longer preoccupied with reproducing God's image from love but instead seeking for self and cut off from love.

The good news is that Jesus came to restore the image of God into mankind and redeem our created value! Jesus made a way for us to have life, intimacy, and relationship forever with the Father, who created our identity in Him. From a place of relationship, we know who we are and we walk in trust, naked and unashamed of who we are. The knowledge of good and evil brings sin-consciousness to the world. Satan and his demons wage war in the heavens to steal, kill, and ultimately destroy our lives and cut us off from the One who loves us. God's desire has always been for us to choose life in Him while reproducing His image, to multiply His love on the earth.

The relationship between Paul and our only daughter, Finley Grace, is an apt illustration. They utterly adore each other. Finley feels no need to hide from her daddy. She knows she is treasured and loved for who she is, on her best and worst days. Paul has solidified her trust in word and action, speaking to her lovingly, holding her, buying her flowers, taking her on dates, giving her affection and attention, and affirming her after she has been disciplined. Their connection is strong, and it's obvious to all who observe their relationship.

For the point of the illustration, let's say the devil whispers to Paul, "You're a bad father. You're not doing enough for your daughter. She questions your love. You're a failure." As a mature follower of Christ, Paul has enough wherewithal, wisdom, and experience to discern a voice other than the Holy Spirit, push aside the devil's lies, and ignore him.

But suppose the enemy then whispers to Finley, "Your daddy doesn't love you. He doesn't think you're beautiful like he says; he's just making that up. He's not proud of you; he didn't really say that. And when you mess up, he slowly stops loving you." Finley would be devastated. She would become more aware of her issues or "sin conscious," and she may begin to perform for Paul, desperately seeking to receive his love despite the fact that she already fully has it. In the worst case, she may cut herself off due to the shame she feels for not living up to the standard of her father's love. The truth is, Paul loves her no matter what she does. It is that simple. And more than that, he is righteously angry when the devil messes with her.

Why does this matter? Finley is being raised in a broken world, whereas Adam and Eve were not. Jesus came to restore what was taken in the garden from Adam and Eve and in turn all of mankind, granting us legal authority in His name to walk in our identity as children of God (1 Cor. 15:45–49). Finley has access to this in Jesus as do you and I. Satan has nothing on God (he is already a defeated foe—see John 16:11), but he continuously attempts to destroy God's children. I imagine it grieves the heart of God when His kids are poked, prodded, assaulted, and attacked by the devil, just as it grieves my heart when my children are bullied or hurt in any way.

In the Garden of Eden, Satan had the ability to encounter Adam and Eve because he was thrown out of heaven to earth (Isa. 14:12–14). He then attempted to usurp God's authority, lying to God's beloved creation, convincing mankind to relinquish our true identity by separating us from our Creator and Father. Adam and Eve chose to receive the knowledge of good and evil over relationship, cutting themselves off from love and exposing themselves to sin and death.

> When the Woman saw that the tree looked like good eating and realized what she would get out of it—*she'd know everything!*—she took and ate the fruit and then gave some to her husband, and he ate. Immediately the two of them did "see what's really going on"—saw themselves naked! They sewed fig leaves together as makeshift clothes for themselves. When they heard the sound of God strolling in the garden in the evening breeze, the Man and his Wife hid in the trees of the garden, hid from God. God called to the Man: "*Where are you?*" He said, "I heard you in the garden and I was afraid because I was naked. And I hid." God said, "Who told you

you were naked? Did you eat from that tree I told you not to
eat from?" (Gen. 3:6–11 Message, emphasis added)

"Who told you that you were naked?" Who told you hiding
from Me fixes your problems? Who told you sex is shameful?
Who told you to try to hide in the darkness from Me? God
knew the answer when He asked Adam and Eve, "Where are
you?" and He knows it for you too. He is waiting for you to
bring the ugly, broken things into the light. He knows who
put shame on you, and He wants to take it off you and wash
you clean. He is asking you, "Where are you?" He wants to
come and meet with you. He made a way to release you from
shame through His Son Jesus, who died naked on a cross,
taking on the shame of the world to have the authority to
reach out and rescue you in any situation.

The point of this story isn't that we shouldn't educate
ourselves or live without knowledge. The point is that God
made us to be with Him, pursue His heart, and reproduce
His image. Adam and Eve were allowed to eat from the tree
of life that they might live forever in communion with their
Creator. But after they had eaten from the forbidden tree,
God sent them out of the garden in His mercy, so that they
would not eat of the tree of life and live sin-conscious forever.
The good news is that Jesus bridged the great divide that sin
produced so that we can again live in constant communion
with our God.

To deceive is to "deliberately cause (someone) to believe
something that is not true, especially for personal gain."[1]
When Satan deceives us, he believes (I think) in his sick and
twisted way that he is gaining some form of personal advantage. I think it's his distorted idea of revenge toward God

because he knows he's defeated and his time is short on the earth. Also, deceived people don't know they're being deceived, and that's how the enemy builds strongholds in our lives—it's a perfect plan on the devil's part to keep God's children in bondage.

My prayer is that your eyes would be opened to any area of your life where you are walking in deception and that you would be set free through God's revelation. And if you can't see it because the deception is so great, I pray there is someone you trust that you will allow to bring truth into your life.

To be a son or a daughter is the most breathtaking gift we've been given. We are no longer slaves to shame, fear, or our past; we are God's beloved children because of Jesus.

After Jesus's resurrection, He appears to His disciples and shows them the scars in His hands and side. He then breathes on them and says, "Receive the Holy Spirit" (John 20:22). This moment is mind-boggling. Why? In the account of creation, what does God do to give life to Adam? "And the LORD God formed man of the dust of the ground, and breathed into his nostrils the breath of life; and man became a living being" (Gen. 2:7 NKJV). God's very breath gave life to Adam—the life that the enemy came to steal. When Jesus was resurrected, overcoming sin and death, his very breath gave the disciples the Holy Spirit—life—and all were redeemed. When we receive Jesus, we receive new life dismantling sin and shame in our lives.

Don't Be That Girl

Lot's wife is a good reminder to each of us about what *not* to do when being delivered from a life of sin and shame.

Sodom and Gomorrah were about to be destroyed because their sin was so flagrant toward God. Abraham had pleaded with God to spare the city if there were ten righteous people living there, and God said he would, but there were not. Abraham's heart was to spare his nephew Lot and his family. God put a plan in place to rescue them, while still taking out Sodom and Gomorrah for their belligerent sin. God was gracious and merciful toward Lot and his family, yet Lot's wife ignored part of the plan of deliverance:

> Lot reached the village just as the sun was rising over the horizon. Then the LORD rained down fire and burning sulfur from the sky on Sodom and Gomorrah. He utterly destroyed them, along with the other cities and villages of the plain, wiping out all the people and every bit of vegetation. But Lot's wife looked back as she was following behind him, and she turned into a pillar of salt. (Gen. 19:23–26 NLT)

God gave Lot and his family a rescue plan: run for the hills and don't look back. God says look ahead to the future, but when we continuously look back at the place of shame God has rescued and healed us from, we become a pillar to our past. Every time people look at us, they remember who we were instead of seeing who we are now. How people see us often has to do with the choices we make that display the fruit in our lives and reveal our belief in who God says we are.

God has given you a rescue plan. He is saying, run toward Him and don't look back. In "the hills" you'll find revelation about who you truly are. He wants to redeem the time and the things that have been devoured and destroyed, but it's impossible for Him to do so if we continuously ignore His instruction and live in disobedience. He has healing for you!

Others may try to build monuments for you and remind you of your past. Remember that they answer to God, not you, for not seeing you as you are. Don't worry about others, judgmental behavior or lack of tact when they converse with you—they need the love of God! Their issues are their issues so don't pick them up.

If you need others' affirmation, then you will strive to win the approval of people and in turn will reject the acceptance from the One who sent Jesus to cover your every sin. God has already put the stamp of approval on your life. When you are covered in the blood of Jesus, God looks at you and sees nothing but a slate that is wiped clean, a son or daughter washed as white as snow. Stop trying to prove that you're clean when you already are.

Sex and Intimacy Free of Shame

Though sexuality is not the only thing associated with shame, it can be one of the most damaging areas of life because of its tremendous kingdom value. Just look at the abundance of sexual abuse, rape, prostitution, perversion, pornography, sadomasochism, and human trafficking in our hypersexualized culture. Sex has been perverted and covered in a blanket of shame. Mud has been thrown all over something that was designed to be beautiful, sacred, fun, and shame-free within the covenant of marriage.

I once saw an ad for a documentary about sex titled something to the effect of "Sex, the original sin." The world has no answer to the broken sexuality that we see, so it seeks to entirely remove shame from the equation, asserting that sin isn't something to avoid. But the original sin wasn't sex; it was taking our own righteousness into our hands. Sex was created to be a beautiful, physical representation of intimacy, which God designed to bring forth life and "create" as He does. In God's eyes, intimacy and reproduction go together; sex was never intended to be "dirty," self-seeking, or perverted. Because of the degree of bondage sexual sin subjects so many to, it's important we touch on it here.

Because of my past, I had no idea how to have beautiful, powerful, and pure sex in the covenant of marriage. I didn't even know it was possible. I talk to many people who think that saving sex for marriage is an outdated concept. Sex as it was designed is not needs-driven—it is a gift to be enjoyed in intimacy, connection, and covenant till death do us part.

Paul and I didn't have sex until our wedding night. It didn't take long to see that we both brought our own baggage and shame to our sexual relationship. We began to cry out to God for wholeness and healing. God has been gracious to bring healing and insight in every season as it has been needed. It's been quite a journey, and it's only gotten better and better. I can honestly say I am blown away at the freedom God has and continues to give us. We are more sexually free and fulfilled today than we have ever been, but we have both been committed to the process.

After we had been married a few years, I heard someone speak about how sex is prophetic, and it caught my attention. Can God be part of sex? Shame makes us think that God is embarrassed about sex, even in the covenant of marriage, and that we should be embarrassed to have Him be a part of it. The truth is that He created it with a very powerful and special purpose and called it good!

In Ephesians 5, the apostle Paul explains that marriage is a "profound mystery" representing Christ (the husband) and His love for the church (the bride). Every time that two come together in the covenant of marriage is a prophetic demonstration of Christ coming back for His Church and becoming one with her. We have yet to behold this profound mystery, because it has yet to take place. It represents the second coming, when the devil and all the powers of darkness will be judged and thrown into the fire of hell forever. Every time you have sex in the intimate covenant of marriage, you are reminding the devil that he is fighting a losing battle. Sex is not just about having a healthy libido; it's also about understanding the power of sex and how it defeats the powers of hell. When it's perverted, it falls straight into the hands of the devil to twist into shame and selfish desires. But truly it is a gift from God to be treasured and enjoyed within the covenant of marriage and to bring Him glory.

The New Has Come

There is healing and freedom for you. Shame is not yours to carry or walk in because it was removed when you were reconciled to God through Jesus Christ: "So from now on we regard no one from a worldly point of view. Though we once regarded Christ in this way, we do so no longer. Therefore, if anyone is in Christ, the new creation has come: The old has gone, the new is here! All this is from God, who reconciled us to himself through Christ and gave us the ministry of reconciliation" (2 Cor. 5:16–18).

Even if it feels like the journey has been long, just keep going. When the enemy comes to say, "Shame on you," hear a whisper resound in your heart "No, my daughter, shame off you!"

Truth: I have nothing to prove and nothing to hide.
God takes me as I am. His love reminds me that my true identity is in Him. I will no longer walk in the shame of my past but in the truth and love that set me free.

▲ ◄ ◄ Walking in Freedom ► ► ▲

1. Grab your journal and sit in a safe place. Ask the Holy Spirit to lead and guide you in your time together.
2. Take a moment and identify obvious patterns of thinking or living that are negatively affecting your life. Ask Father God if these thoughts and ways of living have become pillars to your past shame and pain. Make a list.
3. Now, take that list and find the truth in the Word of God for each of the lies that you have believed. Set aside time to dig into the Bible and listen to the Holy Spirit. You may want to tackle one "pillar of shame" at a time. Be kind to yourself and work at your own pace as you partner with the Holy Spirit. I specifically recommend Psalm 91, which has deeply ministered to my heart and reminded me of my inheritance in God.

4. After you've written down truths, put them up somewhere you will see them every day. Begin to meditate on them and speak them out over your life. Try memorizing one that really resonates with you. You may not feel anything at first. That's okay, truth is still changing you. Do whatever it takes to unearth the treasure that is yours to obtain.

5. As you encounter the healer and lover of your soul, ask what shame you've been holding on to as part of your identity. As a symbolic act, hold that shame in your hands and give it to Jesus. Imagine the love in His eyes as He willingly takes it from you. As you give it to Jesus, ask what He'd like to give you in return. In your mind's eye, put it on and walk in it because it's now part of your wardrobe.

8

Freedom from Control

So if the Son sets you free, you will be free indeed.

John 8:36

Lie: Control keeps me safe and protects my heart from being hurt.

Although I never would have admitted it outright, I used to pride myself on my ability, perceived or otherwise, to control my world and the people in it. I kept an obsessively clean house, with the pillows on my couch so straight that a mere touch from guests would spike my blood pressure. I never missed an appointment or double-booked myself; I was always on top of my schedule. I relished grocery shopping and organizing drawers and cupboards. My living room looked as untouched as a museum with freshly vacuumed rugs aligned to the floor panels and not a single piece of lint visible to the naked eye, poised for *Martha Stewart Living*'s editorial team to show up and shoot a new spread for her magazine. I even meticulously organized our kids' toys, and God forbid they played with *my* toys . . . I would nearly have cardiac arrest. The order made me feel safe, but at the expense of others; nobody was safe if they got in my way.

My control issues were about protecting the compounded years of pain that simply hadn't been given a place to be touched by the healer.

The Tipping Point

Early September 2012, a couple of weeks before our fourth child was born, I was sitting at the counter in our Brooklyn apartment with my mom, dad, brother, and husband talking about the impending birth of Samuel Malachi. I asked the group half-jokingly, "I wonder if having a fourth will push me over the edge to actually deal with my control issues?"

My younger brother, Parker, exploded in laughter, "Yeah, right!!!"

Everyone else laughed uncomfortably at his brutal candor while I smiled nervously, feeling like my life was about to spiral out of control. I'm not a mind reader, but I'm pretty sure my husband was hoping it would push me to change. For years he had been the target of my control issues, which often caused pain and hurt in our marriage. I really did want it to stop, I just wasn't sure how.

Stepping into marriage with a pile of issues (mentioned in previous chapters) as high as it was wide, I grabbed on to the weapon of obsessive control and manipulation and added it to my arsenal. I had never imagined myself married and living in Australia, but I was, and I was out of my depth and out of control at the age of twenty-three. I loved Paul deeply, but I didn't know how to face or deal with the pain that was rising up—so I cleaned obsessively and demanded that my husband do the same. If he didn't, I would give him the silent treatment or the "no sex, don't touch me" treatment, both of which were simply another form of control and manipulation. When our kids came into the picture, I tried to control them too, not because I wanted to but because it was all I knew to do when my life felt as if it was spiraling out of *my* control.

Thank God for the birth of Samuel Malachi, who represented our family's official tipping point. His name means *asked of God, a messenger*, and God sent a clear message with him on the day of his birth. That message was this: "Andi, you need Me. Let Me in. I can heal and restore this area of your life, but only when you decide to stop protecting yourself with control and connect with Me."

The fortress I had built around my heart was quite secure, but it began to be chiseled away by the reality of Sammy in our lives and the work of the Holy Spirit. He needed me. I was his constant source of food and comfort, and he cried just like the rest of the kids, especially when I needed sleep. I felt overwhelmed by the needs presented by all four children.

I was on a four-month maternity leave from our church when, just a week in, Paul was booked to travel on and off for six weeks with only a few days at home between each trip. Unknowingly, I picked up and carried the emotional load of our church while he was traveling and thoroughly stressed myself out. No one asked me to; I just did. It didn't help that at the same time I was trying to figure out how to juggle four children with very diverse, individualized needs, and holding myself to a standard that only Mary Poppins could attain. I felt condemned in my failures, when living a life in Christ carries no condemnation (Rom. 8:1). My stress turned into shingles, which meant I needed medication for the excruciating pain. Each throbbing shot of nerve pain made it nearly impossible to even hold my newborn. The medication made my milk dry up, so I made the unbearable decision to wean Sam at only three months old, when it had been my plan to nurse him for a year. I felt battered by grief on the rocky shores of my present reality. In my mind, I was a total failure.

One afternoon, as I bawled on the sidewalk while pushing Sammy in his stroller with my mom to his three-month checkup, she stopped me, looked me lovingly in the eyes, and pulled me close as I cried. She affirmed me, saying that I wasn't a bad mother and that Sam would thrive on formula. The circumstances simply reminded me that I wasn't in control, and it scared me out of my mind.

The shingles hit right around Christmas, and I was put on bed rest so I could recover. Now, if you're anything like I was, one of the worst things about forced rest is the list you make in your head of everything that's *not* getting done to your standard of perfection. I had an army of people who graciously reached out to help me, but they couldn't do things to my ridiculous standard, and I'm sure I burned a few bridges in the process. Apparently I needed to learn gratitude as well. The help from others was actually threatening everything I was manipulating.

Countless situations during this season pushed my buttons, such as the day I missed something on my calendar and thought it was the end of the world. I was on the road to recovery from the shingles, so I sat down to relax after getting the kids off to school and putting Sam down for a nap. I took my time, read my Bible, wrote in my journal, and enjoyed some peace and quiet. Afterward, I opened my calendar to look at my week and prepare for all that needed to be done in the coming days. To my horror, I saw that I was two hours late to a field trip for which I had signed up to be a chaperone. Zeke's class was well on its way to Harlem, a good sixty-minute subway ride from my home, and I was supposed to be with him! I broke down, shaking violently with sobs of penance and self-pity for the horrible mistake I'd made that I was sure would scar my son for life. My mom and life assistant were at the house and witnessed my panic attack. I couldn't breathe properly nor stop sobbing while wringing my hands to the bone and confessing out loud what I assumed my son thought of his idiot mother. Self-hatred spewed from my mouth as I declared that I was "that mom" who didn't show up, even for her own kid.

I began to run through the list of things I was failing to control, mentally whipping myself. I couldn't feed my own child because I got sick, which was my fault because I couldn't manage the stress I put myself under. I couldn't keep up with my own calendar and remember important dates. I couldn't cook or clean because I was in bed. I couldn't give enough time and attention to each of my children. I had nothing left to give to invest into my husband or the spiritual leadership of the church. I was wretched to be around; I didn't even enjoy my own company.

Pushed to my breaking point, I rose late at night with Sammy while Paul was away in India and wept out my frustrations. At this point, I was quite practiced at throwing pity parties, reminding myself that I didn't measure up and would never be good enough. My tears turned into desperation, and as I sat there looking out over South Brooklyn, I finally cried out to God in a vulnerable and honest moment. I purposefully shaped my worries, fears, shortcomings, and failures into prayer, laying my pain down into my Father's arms like a pile of collected junk. I connected my heart, soul, and mind to the One who had the power to love me and set me free. I was done being the victim.

God, whatever You need to do in me, do it. I'm ready. I want my children's memory of their mother to be one of a woman that can laugh at the days to come. I want to be a woman who actually likes who she is and enjoys her own company. I want my husband not to always be worried about me but to trust in me fully. I want to see and believe that I am of enough value to be healed.

Getting Free

At this point, I turned to Jesus because He was the only option (and the greatest one). I was cornered, and my control had put me there. When circumstance and life happened to me, I spiraled out of control. Now, making myself aware of the presence of God who is always there, I realized how unkind I had been to myself, trying to live at a standard that no human could attain. God's greatest command is that we love Him with all of our heart, soul, mind, and strength, and the second is that we love our neighbor as ourselves (Mark 12:30–31). When we try to live performing for love, we miss the point. The only reason we can love God with all that we are is because He first loved us (1 John 4:19). When we receive that love, it's easy to love . . . to love our neighbor as we love ourselves. The truth is, I didn't like myself, let alone love myself, so performance and control became what I did to feel loved. What hit me was God's absolute loving-kindness and patience with me to let go of control and let Him hold me close. I realized that no one is born a control freak. One learns to become a controller out of a need for protection and some semblance of peace.

Like fear, anger, and shame, control also had become a weapon of choice creeping into my heart when I was three and at the hands of my abuser. This moment fostered a lie that it was unsafe to trust and that I wasn't valuable enough to protect. Add to that an imperfect home (and we've all lived in a version of an imperfect home) coupled with controlling church leadership, and I was in self-protection mode from the moment I can recall memories. Then, as various moments of trauma, rejection, or pain kept rolling in, they solidified my unhealthy belief system. If I couldn't control what happened to me, then I would control my immediate environment in order to feel safe. As I grew up, it came in the form of broken relationships where I had engaged my whole trust in someone who I subconsciously believed would be my savior. This, in turn, hindered me from putting my trust in God. So every time a past boyfriend or my now husband, close friend, church leader, or a situation disappointed me, ultimately letting me down, failing me, or hurting me, there were new reasons to lash out and control my personal world.

Along the way I came into agreement with the lie that "I can do a better job than God. I can protect my heart and life with manipulation and control because it keeps me safe."

Our sovereign God gives us the ability to love Him or leave Him, to let Him into our hearts for communion and deep intimacy or to stonewall Him with a hardened exterior. He honors our decisions, whether with Him or without. Such a gift does not leave room for blaming others for our unwillingness to forgive, let go of our control, and reconnect with our Father. We were created to be face-to-face with Him.

After I chose to surrender my heart, life, and methods of madness to my Creator, the obvious things started to hit me:

- I can't control my husband.
- I can't control my kids.
- I can't control other people's decisions or choices.
- I can't control circumstances.
- I can't control outcomes.
- I can't control painful world events or leaders.
- I can't control what people think or say about me.
- The more I try to control these things, the more I feel out of control and lack peace.

Intentional cultivation of our spirit by connection to the Father, Son, and Holy Spirit will begin to counteract our need to compulsively control our world because it is here that we are loved and in turn can live from love and give love. Here is what I realized I *did* have the power to cultivate in my life through connection to the Holy Spirit:

- I can choose to break agreement with the fear that binds and controls and exchange it for the pure *love* that casts out all fear.

- I can choose to have *joy* and *laugh* at the days to come no matter what season I'm in or what circumstances I face.

- I can choose to pursue and align myself with His *peace* in the midst of the good, bad, ugly, and crazy hectic times in my life. The Prince of Peace came and lives within me, and peace is my inheritance even in the midst of chaos.

- I can choose *patience* when all I want to do is respond in anger and control my environment.

- I can choose *kindness* when my first reaction is vengeance, anger, hatred, or frustration.

- I can choose to rest in the *goodness* of God and the truth that He is a *good* Father even when I see, feel, or experience pain.

- I can choose *faithfulness* on the days I want to throw in the towel and move to a deserted island all alone where no one can talk to me or ever hurt me again.

- I can choose to cultivate *gentleness* when my initial reaction may be brash or harsh because my feelings of pain run deep.

- I can choose *self control* when I want to lash out at those I love and instead bring my deep emotions and pain to God, who will walk me through a process of understanding and healing.

We have the ability to cultivate the fruit of the Spirit because we have been given the Holy Spirit: "And Christ lives within you, so even though your body will die because of sin, the Spirit gives you life because you have been made right with God. The Spirit of God, who raised Jesus from the dead, lives in you. And just as God raised Christ Jesus from the dead, he will give life to your mortal bodies by this same Spirit living within you" (Rom. 8:10–11 NLT).

The fruit of the Spirit is evidence that our hearts are connected to God, the very being of love. Love heals us, and the fruit of our healing is the fruit of the Spirit. The Holy Spirit aids in cultivating what has already been given to us through Jesus's life. The fruit of the Spirit is evidence to me and those around me that the same power that raised Christ Jesus from the dead is alive and at work in me! Our life in the Spirit absolutely transforms us.

Barbie Steps

Paul and I were having breakfast in our boutique hotel in San Francisco on a little getaway when I started to cry over my bacon and eggs. This is normal—both the crying and the bacon and eggs. We had been reading the book *The Supernatural Ways of Royalty*, an insightful teaching on identity, by Kris Vallotton and Bill Johnson. We were talking about the parts that stood out to us when Paul posed a question: "I wonder in what areas of our lives we have a pauper mentality?" It wasn't a particularly emotional question, but it went straight to my heart as I flashed back to memories of growing up.

Some Christmases, when the jobs were coming in for Mom, we were given everything our hearts desired. When things were tight, a box of fresh crayons was the most precious gift received. For me, the one gift that stood out was the annual release of Holiday Barbie. In my mind, if I got a Holiday Barbie, we were rich! On the few occasions that I received a Holiday Barbie as a child, she was so special that she never came out of the box—ever. I was so crippled with fear that she would get ruined and that our family wouldn't have enough money to get another one that I never, ever played with her (and Barbie dolls are meant to be played with, even the collectable ones).

So when my daughter was born in 2008, what do you think I bought her for Christmas? A Holiday Barbie, because I knew from experience that's what a four-month-old desires. I was living vicariously through her, determined she would have a Holiday Barbie each year for the rest of her life, because I hadn't had that. The only problem was that, as she got older, she wanted to open her Holiday Barbie dolls and actually play with them! As a controlling individual, I had visions of crawling into the corner, assuming the fetal position, and rocking back and forth with my ears covered until the questions about opening the Holiday Barbie boxes stopped. My solution was to shove them into the corner of her closet where she couldn't see them and would no longer ask to open them.

Part of my irrational control stemmed from a pauper mentality, or a poverty spirit, and was directly connected to my control issues. Deep down, I was afraid we wouldn't have enough, so what we did have had to be kept safe in case of an emergency (like Toys "R" Us running out of Holiday Barbie dolls, I guess?).

What are you afraid of? Better yet, where in your life are you afraid that you might lose control? Because that is exactly where God wants to come in, hold you, and help close the door of fear in your life—if you'll let Him.

That day in San Francisco I was salting my bacon and eggs with tears, I felt God give me a "Barbie step" to freedom. I heard Him say, "When you get home, the first thing you *could* do is open up all of the Holiday Barbie dolls you've bought for Finley so she can play with them." I noticed immediately that it was a suggestion, not a command. God was reminding me about my choice to take this step into freedom, co-laboring with Him to break the lie I had believed since childhood.

When I got home from that trip, my daughter didn't know what hit her. I took her into her bedroom and pulled down all of the Holiday Barbie dolls from their hiding spot in the closet, including *mine* from the '90s (this was a big deal!). In her excited "Minnie Mouse" Finley voice, she yelped, "Do we get to open the boxes?" I nearly cried. The grace (which is her middle name) she so freely extended to me, even while confronting a troubling experience, began to melt my heart. She wasn't mad at me; she was just excited to be opening the Barbie dolls for the first time. I got the scissors, helped her open them all up, and let her go crazy! I looked her in the eyes and apologized for hiding them from her and asked for her forgiveness. She said nonchalantly, "I forgive you," too distracted by her beautiful Barbie dolls to worry.

I learned so much through that process. I learned that letting go is a daily process; don't be hard on yourself. While you may be delivered in an instant by God's grace during prayer, worship, or elsewhere, more often you will have to make daily decisions that line up with your newfound freedom. For me, it was a "Barbie step." What is it for you?

The funny thing is, from that day forward, I haven't bought Finley another Holiday Barbie (or Barbie in general) because it's not what she likes. Letting go of control also helps us to stop forcing our perceptions of the world onto others.

Continuing in Freedom

Life is lived one step at a time, one day at a time. When you add up your steps along your journey to freedom, you will look back and be amazed at what God has done through your willingness to align with His truth and character. It's what Eugene Peterson called "a long obedience in the same direction."[1] When a moment of freedom takes place, you have grace to run in the revelation that's been given to "go and sin no more" (John 8:11 KJV). The Word says, "The enemy prowls around like a roaring lion seeking whom he may devour" (1 Pet. 5:8 NKJV). The Amplified Bible says, "Be well balanced (temperate, sober of mind), be vigilant and cautious at all times; for that enemy of yours, the devil, roams around like a lion roaring [in fierce hunger], seeking someone to seize upon and devour" (AMP-CE). Don't allow that roaring lion to devour you again. After you receive freedom, you have to get good at saying "You may not." And why do you even have authority to say such things? Because whom the Son sets free is free indeed (John 8:36)! The Son gives you the authority to walk in freedom.

While I, Paul, our son Jesse, and a team from church were on a mission's trip to Zimbabwe, we got to watch a lion feeding take place. It was extraordinary and frightening all at the same time. After we watched them devour a donkey, our group went over to look at another pride of lions that hadn't been fed for days. Jesse, who was only six at the time, was by far the smallest person in our group and, in a lion's eyes, the most vulnerable. We started to notice that one lion in particular, the dominant male, would not take his eyes off Jesse. Wherever Jesse walked, this lion went. When Jesse would crouch down, the lion would roar fiercely and put his paws up on the fence, trying to gnaw his way through the metal to get to my son's tender flesh and feast on him for lunch. Jesse experimented by running up and down along the fence, and the lion followed in step, ignoring the rest of us. His hunger was driving him to aggression. As Jesse's mother, my hackles went up just watching all of this, causing me to go into protection mode even though a gate was between us. I was ready to step in front of my son and take his place on the dinner plate. That lion was literally going to have to step over my dead body before he could touch my Jesse.

Just imagine how God feels when the enemy prowls around you. He gets angry and rightly so! He is so passionate about you, mad about you, and deeply in love with you. The enemy has to "step over" God's one and only Son Jesus to get to you. Read Psalm 18 to see just how fiercely God protects you when the enemy tries to come after you. And realize that when you step into newfound freedom in any area of your life, you've got to guard and protect what God has done within you: "Above all else, guard your heart, for everything you do flows from it" (Prov. 4:23). The greatest guardian of our hearts is the Holy Spirit. We used to protect our hearts and lives with control; now we do so in beautiful partnership with the best bodyguard of our hearts.

But how do we protect this seed of freedom in our hearts in partnership with the Holy Spirit? We need to choose *love* on a daily basis because God's perfect love *casts out all fear* (1 John 4:18), and control is rooted in fear. We need His love as the salve to heal every part of our recovering control-freak heart, soul, and mind. We've got to step into love and put it on like our favorite outfit. Once a moment of deliverance or freedom takes place, it's not surprising to sense fear knocking on the door of our hearts: fear that things will spiral out of control (so it's time to take over again); fear that we won't be protected or covered (so we go back to our old ways of self-protecting with anger and control); fear that life won't turn out how we dreamed or imagined (so we turn from the grace of God and try to earn and control every circumstance in our lives).

Remaining in His love is sometimes as simple as becoming aware of what we already have: "As the Father has loved me, so have I loved you. *Now remain in my love.* If you keep my commands, you will remain in my love, just as I have kept my Father's commands and remain in his love. I have told you this so that my joy may be in you and that your joy may be complete" (John 15:9–11, emphasis added). His love brings great joy in our lives.

Often it's a daily and sometimes moment-by-moment choice to still ourselves and recognize His love. Earlier I talked about choosing to cultivate the fruit of the Spirit instead of choosing to control. Just like sometimes in a marriage to love is a choice (love isn't a ditch you fall into—it doesn't just happen by accident), it's also a conscious choice to remain in the Father's love, especially when we want to wield the weapon of control to protect ourselves. We've got to stop, sit in our Father's lap, and ask ourselves, "Why am I here again?" In that moment of honesty, we can choose to hand the fear over and receive the unending love that covers all, heals all, and protects us.

I'd like to encourage you to let love in. Take time on a daily basis, whether it's five minutes or an hour, to sit in the presence of God and connect with the deeply divine love that longs to infiltrate every area of your life.

Truth: When I live in partnership with and connection to the Father, Son, and Holy Spirit, my heart, soul, and mind have the greatest refuge and fortress. They are safe, and I can trust God with my whole life.

▲ ◄ ◄ Walking in Freedom ► ► ▲

1. Find a safe place for you and quiet yourself. Take a moment and get in touch with how you're feeling—not what you're thinking but what you're feeling. Do you feel sad, lonely, angry, hurt, overwhelmed, weary, or confused? What do these feelings cause you to want to do? Rest in the love of God? Clean compulsively? Punch something or someone? Give up?

2. Now picture God's love. What does that look like to you? What form does it come in? A big blanket to cover you? A deep overwhelming sense of peace? Do you see yourself sitting in the Father's lap? Maybe your feet are dangling in a stream of overwhelming tranquility. Sit and receive His healing love.

3. Ask the Holy Spirit to reveal to you where control became your weapon of choice to protect yourself. Exercise your free will by surrendering control at the feet of Jesus. Then ask the Holy Spirit what He has for you to pick up instead. Write it down.

4. You may be reminded of some people you need to forgive. You may even need to forgive yourself. Take some time to do that now, out loud.

5. How does remaining or abiding in His love change everything when it comes to issues of control? Read John 15:1–17 and study it in your own time. Ask for understanding on how to abide in His love and how this helps you to receive and give love without performance, control, or manipulation. Remember, you don't live *for* love, you live *from* it.

9

Freedom from Isolation

A man who isolates himself seeks his own desire; he rages against all wise judgment.

Proverbs 18:1 NKJV

Lie: Isolation from honest and vulnerable relationships will keep me safe from rejection, betrayal, and pain.

G ood news, your heart is normal!"
Tears filled my eyes as I read those words from my cardiologist while sitting in my office in lower Manhattan. I turned to look out my window, gazing up at the Freedom Tower (as I still like to call it even though its official name is One World Trade Center), laughing and crying at the

same time at the symbolism right outside of my window: freedom.

Two days before, I had been at an appointment with my cardiologist getting an ultrasound to learn whether there were any abnormalities in my heart causing the constant, disturbing heart palpitations I had been experiencing that year. At those times, my heart felt as though someone was holding it in my chest and rattling it around, taking my breath away. Along with the heart palpitations, yet another bout of shingles had erupted on my hip. I felt chained to the reality that my body would react every time we went through a big season. In my head, I knew this was a lie and wasn't in the character of my beautiful, loving God. The counteracting truth is that He sent Jesus to heal my body, my heart, and my mind with resurrection power that is at work within me. Because of this truth, I started to ponder what my responsibility is in partnering with and living in that healing.

Truth be told, it had been a rough year. It was a year filled with much goodness, joy, triumph, celebration, and love, yet the hard and painful things were trying desperately in my head to outweigh all of the good. Heart-wrenching moments kept dancing around in my mind like a creepy circus clown trying to get all of my attention. Friends I thought I would have forever were dropping like flies and stepping out of our lives and into new seasons. I felt rejection set in and started to act as a victim of my circumstances while unhealthy thoughts swirled in my head: *It's not my fault; I'm a target for this stuff; this always happens to me.* My heart was filled with such heaviness that it may as well have been tied to a weight and dropped into the ocean. Subconsciously, I began to isolate myself from connection to others because it seemed safer to detach than to love deeply and be hurt again.

For years, isolation has been a strong tower that I've hidden in during times of pain to separate myself from reality. If I ever felt subject to circumstance, misunderstood, or unable to control others' free will in causing pain to those I love or myself, I'd subconsciously cut them off by drawing an invisible line in the sand because that relationship was now unsafe. For years I allowed what others did to rob my heart of the peace that is my inheritance to walk in, come hell or high water. The problem was, my strong tower was man-made, not God made.

Choosing Loneliness over Potential Pain

Jesus, the Prince of Peace, slept through storms unaffected by fear (Matt. 8:23–27), and because he lives in me, I have access to that peace at all times no matter what others do, say, or think about me. No matter the political or socioeconomic environment. No matter the state of my marriage, the state of the church, the state of the nation, the president that's leading our country, the horrible things I saw on the news today—circumstance does not have the authority to steal my peace and isolate me from love unless I surrender that authority.

Isolating ourselves so we'll never be rejected is simply a different way of being hurt. It's choosing the pain of loneliness over the *potential* pain of loss. By isolating ourselves, we attempt to stop others from rejecting us, but we simultaneously reject the love of God. In turn, we also reject the possibility of thriving in community, friendships, and relationships that are a part of our purpose.

As we consciously choose to move past our desire to self-protect, we go willingly into the pain, hand in hand with the lover of our souls who heals us and keeps us safe in the secret place (Ps. 91:1 KJV). I love those words, "the secret place." The secret place is a secret because it's unknown and untouchable by the enemy and his lies. In the secret place, his lies are broken down and void of power as we discover the truth that sets us free.

Finding Truth

Knowing I needed healing and freedom in this area of my life, I set aside some time to sit with a trusted advisor for a few sessions to pray, get counsel, and move forward.

Through counseling, a few memories instantly came to mind.[1] When I was a young girl, my mom used to overshare with me about her troubles, worries, and pain. I was incapable of processing them or carrying her burdens, but I still felt responsible because I loved her. I realize now that at the time, she was doing her best, and we have so many cherished memories. However, this pattern in our relationship repeated itself for years until underlying resentment set in.

Because I was subjected to these conversations as a child, I unknowingly took the role of the parent, and a huge sense of concern rested on my shoulders. Sitting in a front-row seat and witnessing the pain Dad and Mom walked through, I always felt a sense of responsibility while simultaneously feeling completely powerless to do anything about it. Without even knowing it, an invisible fortress of isolation became my safe place.

I learned in counseling that this is related to something called *attachment-related trauma*. In simple terms, when I would walk into what my head had filed away over the years as unsafe situations, conversations, or relationships, something like a smoke signal would go off in my brain telling my body, "Warning! Unsafe! Abort!" My physical reaction was then to respond with "fight or flight." More often than not, flight was my subconscious response (though sometimes in the case of my unsuspecting husband it was to fight). Isolation became a safe place where I tried to protect my heart and mind in my own strength.

Proverbs tells us that self-protection and isolation are not wise. And not only that, they are also self-serving: "A man who isolates himself seeks his own desire; he rages against all wise judgment" (Prov. 18:1 NKJV).

Jesus stands at the door of our refuge of isolation and knocks (Rev. 3:20), ready to become the One we run to when it hurts so bad we're not sure where to turn. He has the ability to transform our minds (Rom. 12:2) and bind up our broken hearts (Ps. 147:3). Listen: "The name of the Lord is a strong tower; the righteous run to it and are safe" (Prov. 18:10 NKJV).

He wants us to connect deeply with him, hear the truth as we're wrapped in His love, and destroy the lies we've believed. He wants us to connect with others even if it means we could be hurt again because relationship is worth the risk. We are never meant to do life alone.

Overcoming the Orphan Mentality

Isolation breeds an orphan mentality, causing us to merely survive rather than thrive, as we believe the lie that life all alone is safer. When we don't live aware of the life-giving power of Jesus that is working inside of us, we *can* tend to live as orphans abandoned to our circumstances, surviving through each day instead of flourishing in it. Don't get me wrong, sometimes survival is all we have to make it through the pain and loss we've faced. However, there comes a time in life when we have to choose to grow up and do whatever it takes to move forward and live in our freedom.

A woman in our church still on the journey, as we all are, broke down how an orphan mentality affected her life. Over the years that she's been a part of Liberty, I've watched her time and time again commit to the sometimes painful process of breaking lies and choosing to walk in the truth as a daughter of the king, even when she wants to run away to isolate and medicate.

She shared the effects of an orphan mentality:

1. *A sense of being defective*: I felt, and I have used these exact words—"I will never belong to the rest of the human race." I would never be able to relate to "normal" people because I couldn't relate to the experience of a healthy, normal life. It was like being on the outside, always looking in. You feel excluded from humanity.

2. *Lack of identity*: You don't belong to anyone, so where do you get your identity from?

3. *Rejection*: Somehow you didn't make the cut and so therefore were rejected. In turn, you reject yourself and others.

4. *Judgment*: Without a concept of intrinsic worth, you're always trying to prove your worth and therefore end up with an internal scale on which you rank people based

on your perception of their capacity to survive or their likelihood to be socially normal and accepted. Ironically, you're most judgmental of yourself. Most people operating in the orphan spirit are mean to themselves. They may try to cover it up, and therefore appear arrogant, but it is really deep insecurity.

5. *Deep loneliness*: This is undergirded by a lack of capacity to connect to others. It's like you can't feel the love of others because of numbers 1–4. It feels like a wall separating you from others.

6. *Self-defense*: It's you versus the world.

7. *Unhealthy need for affirmation, approval, and attention*: These are all tied to a need for love, but they play out in different ways based on personality types. You may go and do crazy things or perform in order to feel something. You may go in the opposite mode and become super isolationist because it's too painful to feel and you need to shut down.

8. *Fear and shame*: So much shame. You're basically ashamed to be alive and usually have no concept of grace or what the normal parameters for being human and making mistakes are. Every mistake and every failure brings incredible shame because it reinforces that something really is terribly wrong with you. It solidifies the lie you believe that you are actually defective and deserve to be rejected. And then you're just afraid because the world feels very hostile, unwelcoming, and cold through your lens.

9. *Lack of trust*: There is so much confusion going on in your mind, so you just don't believe people. I think

it must be very frustrating to others because it's like pouring water on dry, clay ground—almost nothing seeps in. We dismiss anything positive people say about us because it doesn't align with our core perception of ourselves.

10. *Relationship breakdown*: There is an inability to go to a certain depth, so you either break off the relationship or find ways to destroy it (or move to another city or country) before it gets too close. It's a subconscious decision to reject others before you can be rejected. You literally start convincing yourself the relationship isn't real, the person actually hates you, and it's too good to be true. You just invent it in your mind, and it drives people so crazy they actually reject you. So it becomes a self-fulfilling prophecy.

11. *Emotional flat line*: You harden your heart more and more to protect yourself. I always say it's like feeling in black and white—you don't see the color in life. You also may do crazy things to feel something . . . anything.

12. *A sense of deep injustice*: This can play out as anger or depression (which can be caused by repressed anger) because you feel ripped off by life.

13. *Limited capacity for vision or dreams*: This is tied to a lack of identity. You don't dream because either you don't dare to or you haven't been taught to dream. It's hard to dream when your focus is on lack, and you don't know your inheritance. You feel like you don't have permission to dream because when you feel so rejected, it's an incredible effort to have a voice or to

project anything beyond the level of survival. And then, who will even care?

This may have been hard to read as you possibly identify with one or all of the effects listed above. You may be asking yourself, "Great! So now what?" What *does* this beautiful girl keep on doing? She keeps coming to the table. She keeps showing up to God's table where her Father tells her who she really is, and she keeps showing up to be with the family of God on the earth. Is it always easy for her? No. Is it always easy for any of us? Of course not! But it's worth it.

From Orphans to Family Members

Whatever the enemy's destructive plans have been for your life up to this point, they all aim to orphan you. He wants you living under the law and playing his game, making you think that you're separated from love (but you're not!). This works itself out in countless scenarios in our lives as we look for counterfeits in order to connect and feel something: porn, one-night stands, emotional affairs, picking fights, addictive masturbation, slander, gossiping with others to be in the know, and more.

Don't believe me? Let's look at Galatians:

But when you are brought into the full freedom of the Spirit of Grace, you will no longer be living under the domination of the law, but soaring above it. And what are the cravings of the self-life I'm referring to? They are obvious: Sexual immorality, lustful thoughts, pornography, chasing after things instead of God, manipulating others, hatred of those who get in your way, senseless arguments, resentment when others are favored, temper tantrums, angry quarrels, only thinking of yourself, being in love with your own opinions, being envious of the blessings of others, murder, uncontrolled addictions, wild parties, and all other similar behavior. (Gal. 5:18–21 TPT)

When we are brought into the family, we have a Father who loves us and a Savior who literally died so we never have to (even after we breathe our last—we live!). Death has zero power in our lives! And the Holy Spirit leads us into all truth—*that grace* and undeserved favor call us out of our orphan tower of isolation and into a family. We no longer survive and operate on our own terms. We have an understanding of who we are because of whose we are. In that place, day after day a deeper knowing of our value and worth begins to permeate our entire being. We then understand that we have a place in this big, beautiful picture that is His church—Jesus's bride on the earth. We no longer want to function on our own, outside of grace, doing our own thing. As the Holy Spirit leads us into all truth, we begin to understand that a heart is healed within the dwelling place of connection to love.

For all who are led by the Spirit of God are sons of God. For [the Spirit which] you have now received [is] not a spirit of slavery to put you once more in bondage to fear, but you have received the Spirit of adoption [the Spirit producing sonship] in [the bliss of] which we cry, Abba (Father)! Father! The Spirit Himself [thus] testifies together with our own spirit, [assuring us] that we are children of God. And if we are

[His] children, then we are [His] heirs also: heirs of God and fellow heirs with Christ [sharing His inheritance with Him]; only we must share His suffering if we are to share His glory. [But what of that?] For I consider that the sufferings of this present time (this present life) are not worth being compared with the glory that is about to be revealed to us and in us and for us and conferred on us! (Rom. 8:14–18 AMP-CE)

I *love* this truth! We are sons and daughters of God! Even the fact that there will be pain, trial, and suffering on this earth doesn't compare to the reality that we are fellow heirs with Christ, in life on this earth or in death.

No Longer Slaves

One of my favorite songs of all time is "No Longer Slaves" by Jonathan David Helser and Melissa Helser. This song is a declaration of our freedom and identity in Jesus. It speaks of how we are no longer slaves to fear but children of God, chosen from our mother's womb and brought into a family. His blood—the royal bloodline of Jesus Christ—runs through our veins as a result of being born again, causing us now to be a part of God's family! This reality *should* change the way we live. If it does not, we can simply ask God to open our eyes so that we can find healing in His arms—the arms that we are free to run to at any time as His daughters and sons.

Another beautiful line in the song speaks of God splitting the sea so we could walk right through it into the safety of His rescuing love, alluding to Exodus 14 in the Old Testament when the Red Sea and Jordan River were split for the Israelites so they could leave a life of slavery and wandering in the desert and walk into their promise. In the foretelling sense, it spoke of the sea of sin that would be split in two so that we could always be with the Father, Son, and Holy Spirit in our land of promise and inheritance, becoming who we were always created to be. Jesus spilled his blood, was subject to the horrendous beatings that you and I should have received, and became sin for us. He was obedient to death, the once-and-for-all-sacrifice. The moment he breathed His last breath on the cross, the veil that kept the people from the presence of God in the temple was torn in two (Matt. 27:51; Mark 15:38), symbolizing our access to the Father. We are now the temple of His presence (1 Cor. 3:16–17). Three days after Jesus died, when all hope was lost in humanity's eyes, the Father raised His Son from the dead, making a spectacle of the devil and all the powers of darkness, giving us access not only to Him but also to healing, freedom, and the restoration of all things on this earth as it is in heaven and in the life to come.

The Isolated Heart

Before I got the all-clear from my cardiologist that my heart was normal, a good friend said to me, "There's nothing wrong with your heart, Andi. It's just trying to get your attention. It's saying, 'Hey Andi, hello! I'm here! I'm not switched off. I'm not numb. I'm here. Don't ignore me.'"

Think about it, in the most literal sense, what does the heart actually do? It supplies blood to the rest of the body. Without it we're dead. When arteries are blocked with calcified arterial plaque, we run the risk of a heart attack. The surgery to repair the heart can be performed only by a skilled cardiologist. In coronary bypass surgery, a blood vessel is removed and/or redirected from one area to another to bypass the blockages and restore blood flow to the heart muscle.

You may be trying to fix your heart issues on your own in isolation, but a broken heart is in desperate need of open-heart surgery by the Father because it's on the damaging pathway to shutting down. Our God is capable of much more than a bypass. He can clean, restore, and cause your heart to function the way it was intended, restoring blood flow and life to your entire being. To be set free from isolation and walk in the truth, we have to be willing to do the opposite of what has become habit—intentionally dismantling the lies that we don't belong, that we've been rejected, that we need to be on our own to survive, and so on. This can be done in the arms of God in partnership with a loving community of people who are committed to telling us the truth in love. The heart cannot function on its own. A heart is void of purpose without the rest of the body.

Lying there during the ultrasound of my heart, with doctors measuring every chamber and ventricle, I was in awe watching the strength at which my heart muscle pulsed and pushed my lifeblood to my entire body. The beautiful symbolism of what God was healing within me, within all of us, fills me with wonder and gratitude.

I've learned that trying to manage my stress and pain on my own has at times been a factor in sickness manifesting in my physical body. The truth is, I am not chained to sickness or stress. Relying on myself alone caused me to push down my emotions—compounding heaviness within my heart and in turn breaking out in shingles, staph infections, heart palpitations, depression, and more—instead of bringing them to my healer. To manage something is merely to cope with or deal with it, but God heals us—spirit, soul, and body. He has complete and total wholeness (John 10:10) for us, not just management solutions.

He wants to heal our need to isolate and self-protect if we'll let Him into our fortress. He'd love to be close to you—truth be told, He already is. As an extroverted introvert, I've had to learn the difference between isolation and solitude on my journey to healing. Isolation is painful and lonely, while solitude is what Jesus often sought—He'd steal away to be *with* His Father. It's good to know the difference between isolation and purposeful solitude. Isolation is self-protection from society whereas purposeful solitude is preparation for society. I've learned that it's okay that I like to be alone, that I *need* solitude to thrive within myself and in turn for others. I've also learned that my times of solitude are so much better when I'm aware of the constant connection I have to the One I love.

Truth: I am a daughter, deeply connected to the heart of the Father at all times, and my connection to others in loving community is worth the risk.

▲ ◄ ⊸ Walking in Freedom ⊷ ► ▲

1. Find a safe space; get out your Bible and journal, if you've been using one on this journey. Quiet yourself. Consciously become aware of the presence of God in the room. Settle into that and then audibly invite the Holy Spirit to lead you into all truth.

2. Ask the Holy Spirit if there are any relationships that have made you feel powerless and therefore caused you to step into self-protection in isolation. Isolation can happen even while you're in community and surrounded by people; it's a state of the heart.

3. If you feel ready, repent of protecting yourself instead of allowing Father God to be your fortress and strong tower. Ask for forgiveness and forgive others who have made you feel powerless, rejected, or betrayed. Reference the forgiveness prayer in chapter 4 if needed.

4. Read the whole of Psalm 18 in a translation that you love. Consider the deep love that God has for you. See how powerfully he can protect you, much more powerfully than you can protect yourself. Here is the beginning of that psalm in the NIV: "I love you, Lord, my strength. The Lord is my rock, my fortress and my deliverer; my God is my rock, in whom I take refuge, my shield and the horn of my salvation, my stronghold" (Ps. 18:1–2).

5. Have a plan from here on out for when you are tempted to isolate. (If you don't have a plan, you will naturally go to what has become habitual.) When all you want to do is run away, what will you do instead? Will you first run into the presence of God? Will you keep showing up to the table with those who are in your life? Do you need to seek professional help to partner with the deep work God is doing in you?

10

Keep It Personal

Then, by constantly using your faith, the life of Christ will be released deep inside you, and the resting place of his love will become the very source and root of your life, providing you with a secure foundation that grows and grows.

Ephesians 3:17 TPT

Just a year after we moved to New York City, every Tuesday and Thursday my dad would hang out with Finley while her older brothers were at school so I could have time for pastoral meetings, study, message prep, and whatever was needed to build the church in that season. At the time, Mom and Dad lived up the street from us. Our apartment had beautiful floor-to-ceiling windows, and each day after he'd pick her up I'd watch them walk down the street to my father's house, holding hands and chatting. You could see my father's joy and adoration as he listened to my wispy blonde-haired daughter talk and talk with her little Minnie Mouse voice while wildly gesturing with her free hand.

During the day, they'd do simple things such as laundry, cleaning, cooking, driving the church Suburban to the car wash, and buying a treat at the gas station (because everyone knows that's the real reason you go and fill up your car with gas). It was the simple things that bonded them, and to this day they have such a sweet relationship. We all call my dad Poppy, but Finley calls him Papa. No one told her to do that; their simple yet beautiful connection caused her heart to give him such an endearing name.

There have been times on my journey when I have felt as though I was looking from my floor-to-ceiling windows of life on other sons and daughters who walked in healing with their Father just as I watched my daughter walk down the street with my dad. There were times when I'd look at others' lives and it made me jealous, envious, angry, frustrated, and confused, because I was so far from the freedom I desperately longed for—or so it seemed.

Looking back, I now see how healing those moments with my father and daughter were for me. I wasn't just looking on as they forged a beautiful relationship; I was watching my father walk in his redemptive purpose. Somehow this has been a precious healing salve for my heart, instilling me with hope. This is one reason why community is so powerful. Not so that we can compare our lives to one another, but so we can see what's conceivable through others' victories when maybe we haven't tasted that possibility before.

At a leaders' gathering for our church, Finley came running up to my dad and jumped into his arms, squeezing him tightly and telling him she loved him. He had a twinkle in his eye as he touched her cheek gently and told her he loved her too. His gaze then shifted to me as I adoringly watched them, but he looked heartbroken. In his eyes were tears of regret, not the tears of joy he'd just had for my daughter.

He looked at me with his kind eyes and said, "Andi, I'm so sorry I wasn't there for you like this when you were little."

Unable to hold back the waterworks, I just smiled and said, "Oh Dad, I have forgiven you. So much has been redeemed in my heart just watching you with Finley." We hugged, laughed, and cried, intentionally choosing not to live in regret. Our hearts' desire is to continue to build on a foundation of forgiveness and love as we daily walk in our redeemed relationship.

God often surprises us with His methods and orchestrated moments on the journey to freedom. I wasn't looking or even planning to find healing in my relationship with my father as I watched the bond grow with joyful satisfaction between him and my daughter. Nonetheless, I have received deep healing and freedom along the way. Some of the places and moments you find freedom will stop you in your tracks, move you to tears, and take over your senses. Other times, a simple shift will come almost without effort, until you look back and realize you're different than you used to be. Be open to adventure, wonder, and the unexpected along the way. Our God is deeply personal and knows just what we need.

Change Your Appetite

Along with the element of surprise and adventure comes our choice to make intentional changes that bring freedom. When I went off sugar it wasn't easy.[1] The one thing my body wanted was—you guessed it—sugar! I had to start to feed it things that would detoxify my body and at the same time taste amazing. I called my sister (who is healthy and totally sugar-free) and asked her to send me all of the sugar-free, carb-free dessert recipes she had in her arsenal. After a while of not having any sugar in my body, refined sugar in any form tasted disgusting and way too sweet. It gave me an instant headache and made me sick to my stomach.

Once we change our spiritual appetite, we won't long for nor crave the food from our slavery. But remember, as long as we keep eating the same thing, that's what our bodies will crave. If we eat greasy, fatty fast food, that's what we'll want when we're hungry. If we eat sugar and sweets every day, we'll continue to desire a daily hit of those. We have to consciously choose to taste and see for ourselves that our Father is oh so good.

> The whole Israelite community set out from Elim and came to the Desert of Sin, which is between Elim and Sinai, on the fifteenth day of the second month after they had come out of Egypt. In the desert the whole community grumbled against Moses and Aaron. The Israelites said to them, "*If only we had died by the* Lord's *hand in Egypt! There we sat around pots of meat and ate all the food we wanted,* but you have brought us out into this desert to starve this entire assembly to death." (Exod. 16:1–3, emphasis added)

This Scripture always boggles my mind. The Israelites had just been set free by the very hand of God with signs, wonders, and miracles—an undeniable deliverance. Yet they want to go back to slavery so that they can sit around pots of meat! Personally, I would rather fast in my freedom than die with "good food" in slavery. As long as we stay a slave in our hearts and minds, desiring to eat the "pots of meat" from our past, we'll never taste the freedom and goodness that await us in our promised land—even if it comes with a fight.

Right after the Israelites grumbled about wanting to go back into slavery because the desert was hard and they were hungry, God provided them with manna and quail straight from heaven each day. The manna and quail had a temporary purpose; they were never meant to feast on it for the rest of their lives. It was specifically for the desert season, which was preparation to fight for and take hold of the promised land. There is a season between deliverance and dominion that is called dependence. This cycle of stepping into freedom repeats itself in our lives time and time again: deliverance, dependence, dominion.

God is our deliverer, and He has the ability to free us from any bondage in which we find ourselves. After deliverance, we learn how to walk in dependence on God, understanding that He has all we need to thrive and find strength even if we still find ourselves in the desert. After our appetite has changed and we've received food from heaven and are depending on our God, it's time to partner with Him and step into what is ours. It may require crossing the Jordan at flood stage or silently marching around and around our promise until the walls fall down, and we obtain what's ours. It may look like slaying giants and killing beasts. Or it may look like building a house, tending its garden, and working the fields we've been given. This is what stepping into freedom and taking dominion are like. Those pots of meat we used to sit around and ingest in our slavery don't compare to the feast we'll eat when we get our hands dirty to attain it. I've heard it said, "Opportunity is missed by most people because it is dressed in overalls and looks like work."[2]

Freedom can stay in the promised land too, unattained because it looks like hard work to partner with God and go get it. It looks like waking up with purpose, choosing to rise and sit in the Father's lap, listening for the game plan. It looks like radical obedience when He tells you what to do next, even if it means circling around your promise while people tell you you're crazy. It looks like sleeping through the storm when everyone else is losing their minds. It looks like rolling up your sleeves and jumping in with everything you have.

In our healing, God comes with great deliverance and feeds us manna and quail to strengthen us and change our appetite from eating the meat of slavery. Then the time comes when we're strong enough to go and fight for what's ours in the promised land of our freedom; we don't go in alone.

After the death of Moses the servant of the LORD, the LORD said to Joshua son of Nun, Moses' aide: "Moses my servant is dead. Now then, you and all these people, get ready to cross the Jordan River into the land I am about to give to them—to the Israelites. *I will give you every place where you set your foot*, as I promised Moses. Your territory will extend from the desert to Lebanon, and from the great river, the Euphrates—all the Hittite country—to the Mediterranean

Sea in the west. No one will be able to stand against you all the days of your life. As I was with Moses, *so I will be with you; I will never leave you nor forsake you.* Be strong and courageous, because you will lead these people to inherit the land I swore to their ancestors to give them." (Josh. 1:1–6, emphasis added)

This passage tells us God is *with us*, always. When we're inhabiting our promises and stepping into freedom—He is there. We need only acknowledge His beautiful presence in our lives. And every place where we set our feet, *He will give us!*

What freedom do you desire? What do you want? He is so kind, and He has it for us. We needn't box Him into our way of thinking. He loves us so much that He'll crawl into our boxes with us, but He'd rather bust their walls down and show us the wide-open spaces we're called to live in. His thoughts, ways, and plans for our lives are much more breathtaking than we can imagine.

How Will You Respond?

When I was battling jet lag in South Africa, this particular line kept repeating itself in my mind and heart while I was trying to fall asleep: "Responsibility is your ability to respond. Responsibility is your ability to respond. Responsibility is your ability to respond. . . ."

Around and around it went as the Holy Spirit tried to bore something deep inside of my heart. I shot up in my bed, "Okay! I hear you! I'm responding! What do you want to say to me?" For nights on end, God began to download several things into me, and all of them went straight back to the position of our hearts.

God has made us powerful: powerful enough to receive or reject Him, powerful enough to walk with or without Him, powerful enough to respond to Him and His words or not. It comes down to our free will and what or whom our will is submitted to—our way or God's way? He has endless freedom for us, but will we step into it?

You see, our heart issues and the state of our hearts are completely our responsibility. We'd like to blame those around us, our circumstances, upbringing, environment—and even God—for our not flourishing in life. But the truth is, we are responsible for the state of our hearts. Out of the abundance of the heart, our mouths speak. So, what's been coming out of your heart? Whatever bubbles out of your mouth reveals what is deep within you (Luke 6:45).

Our hearts are likened to a garden that we have the responsibility to tend. Don't believe me? Well, take Jesus at his word then.

> Listen! A farmer went out to plant some seeds. As he scattered them across his field, some seeds fell on a footpath, and the birds came and ate them. Other seeds fell on shallow soil with underlying rock. The seeds sprouted quickly because the soil was shallow. But the plants soon wilted under the hot sun, and since they didn't have deep roots, they died. Other seeds fell among thorns that grew up and choked out the tender plants. Still other seeds fell on fertile soil, and they produced a crop that was thirty, sixty, and even a hundred times as much as had been planted! Anyone with ears to hear should listen and understand. . . .

Now listen to the explanation of the parable about the farmer planting seeds: The seed that fell on the footpath represents those who hear the message about the Kingdom and don't understand it. Then the evil one comes and snatches away the seed that was planted in their *hearts*. The seed on the rocky soil represents those who hear the message and immediately receive it with joy. But since they don't have deep roots, they don't last long. They fall away as soon as they have problems or are persecuted for believing God's word. The seed that fell among the thorns represents those who hear God's word, but all too quickly the message is crowded out by the worries of this life and the lure of wealth, so no fruit is produced. The seed that fell on good soil represents those who truly hear and understand God's word and produce a harvest of thirty, sixty, or even a hundred times as much as had been planted! (Matt. 13:3–9,18–23 NLT, emphasis added)

The purpose of soil in agriculture is to receive the seed until it grows into its intended matter and serves its purpose on the earth, whether it's vegetation, trees that produce oxygen, food, or the like. If our hearts are likened to soil, then their purpose is to receive the seed that God scatters among us through His word, messages we hear, time with Him, listening to His voice and heartbeat, godly leadership, and so on. The state of our hearts determines the well-being of the seed and its ability to produce thirty, sixty, or one hundred times the DNA that is within that seed. God wants to entrust us with more, but we a have a responsibility to tend our hearts.

If we continue to wallow in unforgiveness, bitterness, or offense without confronting the issues God has been allowing to come to the surface of our hearts for weeks, months, or even years (because He gives us the grace to deal with them in each season), or while reading this book, our hearts will begin to harden. This is where self-protection sets in. Then, when "seed" is scattered onto our lives, we despise and reject it, not understanding all that God wants to give us.

When we cultivate and take responsibility for our hearts, God can entrust us with more. Often we just have to wake up to the ability and respond. We can respond to life with:

- Forgiveness—canceling a debt that someone owes us spiritually, physically, mentally, or emotionally that they will never be able to pay.
- Repentance—turning from our way and truly submitting our *whole* life (not just our big toe) to God.
- Gentleness—to be kind, not harsh.
- Patience—"The capacity to accept or tolerate delay, problems, or suffering without becoming annoyed or anxious."[3]
- Love—the standard at which Jesus gave His life for us, and the standard we are required to give to one another.

We have the ability to respond to:

- His goodness—It's His goodness that leads us to repentance, rather than rules, law, expectations, or regulations.
- His invitation—He invites us into relationship and a life that flourishes.
- His call—Don't feel like you have a call? Just respond to Jesus's famous last words and you'll change the world: "Go and make disciples!"

- His invitation to rise up—Whether we feel like it or not, it's our responsibility.

- His love—I always say "Loved people love people," so will we let God love us? He longs to have every part of our hearts.

- His gifts and generosity—Everything we have is a stewardship responsibility, so how will we respond to what He has placed in our hands: children, money, gifts, abilities, time, family, relationships, and so on?

- What happens to us—This one is hard because so many difficult, painful, and terrible things have happened to many of us, potentially hardening our hearts. Will we partner with God to soften our hearts? Facing the pain and choosing to forgive and receive love is key, even if we don't feel like it.

- His Word—God has given us so much in and through His word, but how will we respond to it?

- Fear—Yes, fear. Will we let it rule us or will we respond with faith and love?

And so much more.

Consider Abraham and Sarah. Abraham's response to his wife's negativity and unbelief in the seeming delay of God's promise of a son brought them Ishmael before they had Isaac. One child represents their way, the other child represents God's way, and both had to do with their response to a promise.

In our lives, are we producing Ishmaels or are we allowing God to bring about Isaacs? Are we going our own way or are we willing to take the time to cultivate our hearts and bring about the good things God desires to produce in our lives that will have lasting generational impact? We are responsible.

Keep It Personal

Each summer we take a month off and go on vacation as a family to refresh, rest, connect, and have fun. On the last night of our 2016 family vacation in Hawaii, tears filled my eyes and spilled down onto my pillow as beautiful memories filled my heart and flashed before my eyes. I lay there recalling the tender, fun, silly, breathtaking, life-lesson and heart-connection moments with my family, and I couldn't help but smile, laugh, and cry all at the same time. So many emotions filled my heart: sadness and grief that it was over until next year; joy at all the laughter and fun moments we shared; the realization that my kids are growing up *so* fast! Each vacation marks a tender time in our lives—where we enjoy the moment, bid farewell to what has been, and embrace what is to come. While on vacation, our kids have all learned to swim; Sammy has perfected the cannonball. We enjoyed hikes, waterfalls, good food, funny jokes, long games of Monopoly, too many burgers and hot dogs to count, Shirley Temples at sunset, salty skin, sand castles, swimming in the gentle, warm waves of the ocean, finding creatures on the rocks, bird watching, too many Disney Channel shows to count, and of course, cuddles and kisses without end. These times together are intentional and deeply personal for our family, filled with memories that we talk and laugh about in the days, weeks, months, and years to come.

Just like the connection to my family and my memories are deeply personal, so is your life. It's personal. Your freedom journey is deeply personal. The memories you create with the Father, Jesus, and Holy Spirit are personal, real, and raw. Your feelings are personal. Your pain is personal. Your relationships are personal. Your life is personal. This book, right now—for you, it's personal. God has always been personal; you'll find that He's closer than the air you breathe if you just acknowledge His presence. Jesus is deeply personal—His breathtaking sacrifice, exchanging your life for His, can't get more personal. The Holy Spirit, our gift from heaven, is so beautifully personal and always present.

Recall and recount what God has personally done in and with you throughout the pages of this book.

Look at how much encouragement you've found in your relationship with the Anointed One! You are filled to over-flowing with his comforting love. You have experienced a deepening friendship with the Holy Spirit and have felt his tender affection and mercy. (Phil. 2:1 TPT)

And there's more where that came from! Keep it personal. Keep it real. Keep it raw. Keep it honest. Keep Jesus and His love at the center.

When we relegate our lives to empty, impersonal, self-protecting transactions lacking engagement and connection, we can expect fear, rejection, insecurity, and confusion to play with our minds and mess with our hearts as we camp out in isolation within our man-made strong tower of choice. Unforgiveness, fear, anger, shame, control, and isolation are all man-made fortresses in partnership with lies from the pit of hell that build walls around our hearts and lives. We need to let the healer close enough to break down those walls and in turn become our shelter and safe place. The enemy would love us to depersonalize everything and to keep us separated from true connection and love, fearing constant pain, and believing the lie that healing is for everybody else. Keeping it personal is so important.

We've all been in conversations, maybe during a break-up or when being turned down for a job, when someone has said to us, "Don't take this personally but . . ." Maybe in that moment it took everything in you to hold back the tears, choke down the deep sadness rising up, and push back your feelings in an effort not to show your true hand because for you, it was and is personal. It hurts. It causes your mind to go down roads that lie to you and tell you that you're not good enough, that you're not worthy, or that you don't carry any significance on this planet. Why? Because life *is* personal no matter how many people tell you not to take it that way. And God is personal. In fact, He is wild about you to such immeasurable depths that it's literally incomprehensible (Eph. 3:18).

How do you learn the truth about the lies that have held you captive and live free? Be found in the arms of the Father, the One who has all authority over the accuser. There, "the life of Christ will be released deep inside you, and the resting place of his love will become the very source and root of your life, providing you with a secure foundation that grows and grows" (Eph. 3:17 TPT).

The healer mends our hearts and lives in countless moments of significance and seeming insignificance. Moments like watching my dad walk down the street holding my daughter's hand. The moment when my husband reached out and pulled me into his arms to dance with him at his fortieth birthday, when he hates to dance but knew how much it meant to me; in one beautiful and humble moment, he simply yet powerfully reinforced his love and preference for me. Healing has come from the soft touch of my four-year-old stroking and kissing my face for no other reason but love, and in eye-opening moments in prayer sessions when time seemed to stand still. It has been in the tenderness of a friend's hand on my back when it seems like all is falling apart. And in the hot tears hitting my comforter in the midnight hour when the only arms holding me are unseen by the naked eye but seen and felt with the eyes of my heart.

These deeply personal times are the simple yet profound moments that take our breath away and make all things new as we continue to put one foot in front of the other, day in and day out. They are raw, real, honest, dripping snot, tear-filled moments when the darkest night of our soul is chased away by the light of truth wrapped in a beautiful package of love. Where heaven's embrace wraps around us here on earth from our deeply personal, closer-than-the-air-we-breathe, tenderhearted, compassionate God as the life of Christ is released deep inside of us. He holds us to His chest and declares with explosive authority and power to the enemy of our soul as we rest in the safety of His protective, strong arms: "You cannot touch her here. *She is free.*"

Appendix

Receiving the Gift of Salvation

God wants you to thrive and walk in wholeness and freedom. He has made a way for you to be His daughter, adopted into His family through the life, death, and resurrection of His Son, Jesus, so that you can step into all He has for you. In Him is everything you need to walk in freedom. Maybe you've been trying to find your way, discover what truth is and the meaning of life, but Jesus comes to us and says, "*I am the way and the truth and the life*. No one comes to the Father except through me" (John 14:6, emphasis added). He is the way to follow, the truth you've been seeking, and the fullness of life that makes all things new.

Jesus, who was before all things and in whom all things are held together (John 1:1–3), came to earth as a man; the Word became flesh and "moved into the neighborhood" (John 1:14 Message). Jesus became sin for us so that we could become the righteousness of God (2 Cor. 5:21). He was a perfect sacrifice (Heb. 9:14), willingly laying down His life (1 John 3:16) on a cross so that we could be born again—literally born from God by the receiving of his Holy Spirit (John 3:1–21). When we confess with our mouths and believe in our hearts that Jesus is Lord (Rom. 10:9), not only are we born again, we also receive His Holy Spirit, the guarantor of our salvation—that is, a down payment of our eternal life (John 14:15–31; 20:22)! We have the privilege of entering into His divine family as an adopted daughter of God. Everything that is God's becomes ours. Everything that held us back from speaking to God face-to-face is stripped away.

When we choose to turn from our own ways, surrender our lives and ways of thinking, and make Jesus Lord and Savior of our eternal souls, we are reconciled into the family of God. Salvation is a gift that Christ paid for on the cross that we receive for free because there is nothing we could have done in our own efforts to earn or deserve it. It is a gift that is freely given because of God's great love for us. Through the cross and resurrection, Jesus rescued us from eternal separation from Himself (hell, death, darkness, and pain!) by bringing us into His light and love. We are a new creation (2 Cor. 5:17)! He transforms us daily to become more like Him as we choose to continually commune with Him and abide in His love (John 15:1–8).

If you'd like to receive the gift of salvation through Jesus's death and resurrection, please pray this prayer out loud as you confess with your mouth what you believe in your heart to be true (Rom. 10:9–10):

Father, I thank You for loving me and leading me to truth. I am sorry for living life my own way. I

*acknowledge that I have sinned and have fallen short
of Your standard by toiling for my own protection and
provision, living by my own self-righteous standard. I
believe that You sent Your Son Jesus, born of a virgin,
who lived a perfect sinless life, to die for me and carry
my guilt, sin, and shame on the cross. I believe that He
rose again on the third day after He died, conquering
sin and death, and then was seated at Your right hand.
I believe that because of His sacrifice and resurrection,
I am able to enter into a right and loving relationship
with You, Father God. I now confess Jesus as my Lord
and Savior.*

*I thank You that I am now a new creation, born again
and walking in Your resurrection power and love daily.
Fill me with Your Holy Spirit so that I may be led into
all truth. I no longer live for myself; I live for You, with
You, and in You. Thank You for loving me and for Your
grace that enables me to walk with You daily.*

My whole life is Yours. Amen.

Congratulations! I wish I were there with you to celebrate
this moment! Heaven is celebrating your homecoming! Here
are some next steps you can take to help you thrive on this
new journey of discovery and reconciliation:

- Tell someone that you just made this decision, prefer-
  ably a follower of Jesus who can walk alongside you.
- Be baptized. This is a public declaration of a private
  decision between you and God and acts as a prophetic
  act of receiving a clean conscience.

- Actively try to find a healthy church community where you can demonstrate to others the love you've received. (Recommendations on what to look for are below.)
- Consider purchasing a new Bible for yourself and start reading it today and then everyday for the rest of your life. I recommend possibly starting in the book of John because he constantly called himself "the one whom Jesus loves." He was a passionate follower of Christ who had a healthy sense of identity, and so should we!

How to Identify a Safe and Healthy Church Community

I understand that the process of discovering a healthy, thriving, life-giving church community isn't always easy. Community has been essential for me in the journey of healing. No church is perfect, but doing life alone was never how we were designed to live.

The purpose of the church is to equip the saints—you and me (Eph. 4:11-13), because we have been given the ministry of reconciliation (2 Cor. 5:19–20). We gather to spur each other on to love and good works (Heb. 10:24–25) and to worship God corporately in spirit and truth (John 4:23–24).

A healthy church community should resemble a family. You don't always have to agree, but love is the foundation of your service and relationships. Just like a healthy human body, a hand cannot exist apart from the arm, which cannot exist apart from the neck, and so on (1 Cor. 12:12–27). It's good to note that the church is not *just* coming together on a Sunday as we have been conditioned to believe—it is a body that functions together week in, week out. We don't just *go* to church, we *are* the church, and together we are the chosen vehicle to reconcile the world to their Creator and Father God. The church is the one thing that Jesus proclaims the gates of hell cannot prevail against (Matt. 16:18)! Sunday worship or corporate gatherings are simply and powerfully a place for equipping, stirring each other up in love and good works, and activating us to live a gospel-centered life Sunday through Saturday. With that in mind, we don't gather on Sunday only for what we can *receive* but also for what we can *give* to one another.

While this is not an exhaustive list, here are a few things to consider when searching for a healthy church community to do life with:

- Biblically based
- Christ centered
- Gospel centered and disciple making
- Outward looking—missional
- Balance of truth, grace, and love in teaching and environment. An environment that is out of balance oftentimes negates the full gospel and causes extremes in the environment, which can be damaging
- Cultivation of community in some way, shape, or form, whether through discipleship/mentorship groups, serving alongside others, Bible studies, community transformation, or the like (one that is not just Sunday focused because it becomes easy to hide and simply attend church rather than become part of a faith community that can challenge, uplift, and walk with you through every season)

- Evidence of genuine, healthy friendships in the community and in leadership
- Evidence that the lives of the leaders align with their message by example and integrity
- Ability of every person to come as they are, regardless of past or present circumstances or appearance and without fear of judgment or shame
- A place where you feel safe and would want to bring your neighbor, friends, and family

What to Look for in a Counselor or Therapist

There may be seasons in our lives when we need professional help in partnership with what God is already doing in our hearts. Let me just say that there is no shame attached to that decision. Here are a few helpful things to consider:

- Are they Christian? When you are receiving professional help that has its foundation in the same biblical truth and understanding as what you are already working on internally, there is potential for more open and trusting communication. This is my personal conviction, but not everyone would agree; this can depend on various factors for each individual.
- Check what their areas of specialty are—for example, marriage and family, addiction, eating disorders, sexual abuse, and so on—and select according to your individual need.
- Try them for at least three sessions, and don't be afraid to look into other options if you don't feel comfortable or do not feel as though they can really help you.

- A note: remember that a counselor or therapist is not your savior. They are there to come alongside you to help facilitate freedom. If you start to feel like you *need* them, or if *they* make you feel like you need them to go on in life, talk to a trusted friend to get advice as to how to move forward. Remember, Jesus has everything you need to live and walk in freedom. He has done it all.

She Is Free Conference

We'd love to have you at our annual She Is Free Conference in New York City. Please go to www.sheisfree.com for more details and to register. We exist to equip and activate women to walk in freedom and see others set free. She Is free creates a safe and intimate environment where women can encounter God, experience personal transformation, and step into freedom—spirit, soul, and body.

Acknowledgments

Dad and Mom, if you hadn't fought for freedom in your own lives, where would any of us be? The two of you have held me more times in my adult years than I ever allowed you to in my younger years. Each one of those moments has brought so much healing and restoration. Our spiritual inheritance is breathtakingly beautiful, and I love walking in redemption with you. Thank you for saying yes to healing, yes to Jesus, yes to New York, and for becoming the redemptive picture of what a father and mother are to countless lives. I love you both more than words.

Paul, thank you for simply letting me be me. For always allowing me the room I need to be vulnerable, to process, and to deeply feel. It is an act of love. Your patience and kindness help bring about wholeness in my heart on a daily basis. You truly exemplify the steady love of Jesus in my life. Thank you for sticking by me and loving me when I'm hard to be around. Thank you for cheering me on and constantly propelling me forward, further than I ever thought I could go. Thank you for constantly telling me that I *am* smart, I *can* write, and I *do* have something to say even when I believed the opposite to be true for so many years. For the record, I now believe you.

To the joys of my life: Ezekiel Benjamin, Jesse Freedom, Finley Grace, and Samuel Malachi. Every single one of your births has been a prophetic declaration of God's kindness, faithfulness, and love. Your lives constantly teach me and cause me to run into the arms of Jesus to be a better momma, wife, friend, leader, and woman. Thank you for all the times you have given me space to work on this book so I can sow seeds of freedom into the lives of others. This is your inheritance too. Thank you for always asking questions about how the writing is going with genuine interest. I love living life with every single one of you, and I am honored and proud that I get to be your momma.

Justin and Kristin, thank you for taking me to church every Sunday when I was nineteen and living in a dorm room at UW in Seattle. My heart was broken and so far away from God, and you just kept showing up even when I wished you wouldn't. Your faithfulness, love, and consistency in my life, to this day, have brought healing to my heart time and time again. You are not just my family, you are true friends.

Tom and Camille, thank you for giving me "that journal" on my thirtieth birthday during one of the hardest seasons of my life. I'm sure you remember that on the front of it is a picture of me on the day of my birth in the arms of Mom and Dad. It was so beautiful and you had written on it that it was dedicated to "my book" that I would one day write. Well, here it is. You guys have consistently believed in me and loved me and are truly two of my best friends, heart of my heart; distance has not and never will change that.

Parker and Jessi, thank you for jumping in the pit with me time and time again. For being strong and bold enough to confront me because you love me. For really seeing me when so many people just needed something from me. For telling me the truth when I'd get wrapped up in fear, lies, or circumstance. I love you so much.

Liberty Church, thank you for being our family. You were more than worth leaving everything we knew at the time to sow a seed into New York City in hopes that it would grow into beautiful communities that would transform lives with the unstoppable love of Jesus. You are a huge portion of my "why," my inspiration, passion, and a big reason I continue to run into the arms of the Father on a daily basis. I want to lead, come alongside you, and love you well always. May we continue to live honest lives together in loving community that brings renewal to cities and nations.

To every woman who assembles in New York City under the banner of freedom at the She Is Free Conference each year. Continue to carry your freedom in your hands, get dressed in it, and walk uncompromisingly in it as if you're on the runway of life—because you are. And then never, ever stop giving it away. We are free to set others free.

To all the women who have inspired me, sown into my life, and paved a way that propelled me and countless others forward. There are too many to count, but to name a few: Lisa Bevere, Wendy Treat, Linda Sharkey, Bobbie Houston, Darlene Zschech, Christine Caine, Nancy Alcorn, Sharon Kelly, Valery Murphy, Holly Wagner, Charlotte Gambill, and so many more. You have all been mentors and/or mothers in the faith to me even from afar, and I wouldn't be where I am today without you.

To Jenn Harding for being one of the first out of the gate to tell me I should write a book and then showing me how; you were a catalyst to get this ball well and truly rolling.

To Mike Kai, my Hawaiian brother from another mother who over the years, every time I saw you would ask, "How's the book going?" even if I wasn't writing a thing. And to Lisa Kai, my friend, your constant encouragement, steady love, and real friendship have been life giving since that first long car ride when we connected like a house on fire. I am forever grateful for you.

Dawn Sadler, thank you for the constant poking, prodding, structural advice, and writing marathons that caused me to make room for the gift. You helped bring this book into existence. You inspire me more than you know.

To Dominika Wilk for reading each chapter in its raw form at the most random of times. For loving our family well and giving me margin to write, write, and write some more. We love you!

Trisha Schrader, thank you for organizing my life, listening to me verbally process even when I'm sure you had so much work to do, and loving me well on this emotional journey. You are a beautiful friend and steady warrior.

Enid Bozic, thank you for taking the time to help me get a proposal ready for possible publishers. Your input and constant encouragement was fuel for the fire.

Tyler and Hannah Pines, thank you for the invaluable feedback on the manuscript before I sent it off to my editors. Our times together at your kitchen table helped shape this book.

Jamie Chavez, your input in that first round of edits taught me so much! Thank you for saying yes to partnering with me and making me a better writer.

To Lucas Gifford and Christa Black-Gifford for being two of the most real, raw, deep, fun, amazing friends that have walked along the journey over the past few years.

Jana Burson, thank you for taking a chance on me when I was unknown and a total long shot in the publishing world. Your belief in me and absolute brilliance to coach, teach, and guide me along this journey has opened doors in my life I never thought I'd walk through. Because of it, seeds of freedom are being sown into the lives of those who are longing for more.

Rebekah Guzman, thank you for really seeing me, hearing my heart through the pages of the proposal, and helping me shape and hone my voice. Your encouragement and coaching throughout the editing process has been priceless. You are a gift.

Baker Books, your belief in me has blown my mind. I am so honored to be on this journey with you; you're now forever a part of my family.

To My Father, to Jesus my Healer and Friend, and to the Helper—thank you for taking me by the hand and walking with me in and through every season of life. For being faithful, kind, and true . . . for being the Love incarnate that has healed my heart, soul, body, and mind. Thank you for teaching me to write with You and not for You. I am not Your performer; I am Your daughter and friend. This book is Yours and wouldn't exist without You. When all is stripped away, You are truly all I want and need. I love You.

Notes

Chapter 1 Trapped by Pain

1. Oswald Chambers, *My Utmost for His Highest*, in *The Complete Works of Oswald Chambers* (Grand Rapids: Discovery House, 2000), September 10.

Chapter 4 Freedom from Unforgiveness

1. Robert H. Thune and Will Walker, *The Gospel-Centered Life: Study Guide with Leader's Notes* (Greensboro, NC: New Growth Press, 2011), 67.

2. Famous Michelangelo Quotes, Michelangelo Gallery, http://www.michelangelo-gallery.com/michelangelo-quotes.aspx.

Chapter 5 Freedom from Fear

1. *English Oxford Living Dictionaries*, s.v. "authority," https://en.oxforddictionaries.com/definition/authority.

2. Charles Spurgeon, "Psalm 103," in *The Treasury of David*, The Spurgeon Archive, accessed October 20, 2016, www.romans45.org/spurgeon/treasury/ps103.htm#expo, emphasis original.

Chapter 6 Freedom from Anger

1. James Strong, *A Concise Dictionary of the Words in the Greek Testament with Their Renderings in Authorized English Version* (Cincinnati: Jennings & Graham, 1890), 72.

2. HELPS Word Studies, copyright © 1987, 2011 by H.E.L.P.S. Ministries, Inc., thediscoverybible.com/features/word-studies.

Chapter 7 Freedom from Shame

1. *English Oxford Living Dictionaries*, s.v. "deceive," https://en.oxford dictionaries.com/definition/deceive.

Chapter 8 Freedom from Control

1. Eugene Peterson, *A Long Obedience in the Same Direction: Discipleship in an Instant Society* (Downers Grove, IL: InterVarsity, 1980).

Chapter 9 Freedom from Isolation

1. Out of honor for my mother, I've asked her permission to share this next part of the story. I love my mom more than I could ever say, and our relationship has shown me that restoration is more real than the air we breathe if we continually commit to the journey with one another.

Chapter 10 Keep It Personal

1. I would be remiss if I failed to mention that simply taking care of our physical bodies helps too. There's a clear connection between physical, emotional, and mental health. Exercise and eating right can clear away a lot of the brush on our paths to spiritual freedom.

2. Quote attributed to Thomas Edison.

3. *English Oxford Living Dictionaries*, s.v. "patience," https://en.ox forddictionariees.com/definition/patience.

Andi Andrew was born and raised in Spokane, Washington, and in 2002, she met, fell in love with, and married her husband, Paul, in Sydney, Australia. Her first three children were born on Aussie soil. In 2010, her family packed up their lives and moved to NYC to establish Liberty Church, now a growing church with multiple communities, representing forty different nations, in the city and beyond. Paul and Andi currently reside in Brooklyn, New York, with their now four children (three boys and a girl): Ezekiel (Zeke) Benjamin, Jesse Freedom, Finley Grace, and Samuel Malachi.

Andi is passionate about seeing people rise up, walk fully in the truth, and step into their God-given identity. Freedom is her passion, as she has personally been set free from so much through the relentless love of Jesus. She desires to compel others to step into the freedom that they have access to in Christ—spirit, soul, and body. It's one of the big reasons why she launched the She Is Free Conference in the spring of 2015 in the heart of NYC.

Currently, Andi's life is focused on raising her young family, copastoring Liberty Church alongside her husband, Paul, writing, and traveling and speaking to different churches all around the world.

STAY CONNECTED
WITH THE
AUTHOR

 ANDI
ANDREW

ANDIANDREW.COM
FACEBOOK.COM/ANDIANDREW
INSTAGRAM @ANDIANDREW

WE EXIST TO

EQUIP AND ACTIVATE

WOMEN TO WALK IN FREEDOM
AND SEE OTHERS SET FREE.

The She Is Free Conference creates an intimate
environment where women can step into freedom—
spirit, soul, and body.

SHE IS FREE®

SHEISFREE.COM
@SHEISFREENYC
#SHEISFREENYC

✳ LIBERTY*church*